Housing in Developing Cities

Universally, the production, maintenance and management of housing have been, and continue to be, market-based activities. Nevertheless, since the mid-twentieth century virtually all governments, socialist and liberal alike, have perceived the need to intervene in urban housing markets in support of low-income households who are denied access to the established (private sector) housing market by their lack of financial resources.

Housing in Developing Cities examines the range of strategic policy alternatives that have been employed by state housing agencies to this end. They range from public sector entry into the urban housing market through the direct construction of ('conventional') 'public housing' that is let or transferred to low-income beneficiaries at sub-market rates, to the provision of financial supports (subsidies) and non-financial incentives to private sector producers and consumers of urban housing, and to the administration of ('non-conventional') programmes of social, technical and legislative supports that enable the production, maintenance and management of socially acceptable housing at prices and costs that are affordable to low-income urban households and communities. It concludes with a brief review of the direction that public housing policies have been taking at the start of the 21st century and reflects on 'where next', making a distinction between 'public housing' and 'social housing' strategies and how they can be combined in a 'partnership' paradigm for the 21st century.

Patrick Wakely is an independent consultant and Professor Emeritus of Urban Development in London University and former Director of the Development Planning Unit (DPU), University College London (UCL). An architect (AA Dipl, London), he has 40 years of experience of research, consultancy and teaching in housing, planning and urban development, on which he has worked in more than 20 developing countries.

Housing in Developing Cities
Experience and Lessons

Patrick Wakely

Routledge
Taylor & Francis Group

NEW YORK AND LONDON

First published 2018 by Routledge
52 Vanderbilt Avenue, New York, NY 10017

2 Park Square, Milton Park, Abingdon, Oxon, OX14 4RN

First issued in paperback 2019

Routledge is an imprint of the Taylor & Francis Group, an informa business

Library of Congress Cataloging-in-Publication Data
Names: Wakely, Patrick, author.
Title: Housing in developing cities : experience and lessons /
    Patrick Wakely.
Description: New York, NY : Routledge, 2018.
Identifiers: LCCN 2017048314 | ISBN 9781138572089 (hardback)
Subjects: LCSH: Low-income housing—History—20th century.
Classification: LCC HD7287.95 .W35 2018 | DDC 363.509173/2—dc23
LC record available at https://lccn.loc.gov/2017048314

ISBN: 978-1-138-57208-9 (hbk)
ISBN: 978-0-367-22028-0 (pbk)
ISBN: 978-1-351-21239-7 (ebk)

Typeset in Times New Roman
by Swales & Willis Ltd, Exeter, Devon, UK

Contents

List of Abbreviations and Acronyms   vii
Foreword by John F.C. Turner   x
Preface   xiii
Acknowledgements   xvi

1   Informal Housing Procurement Processes   1

*1.1 The Informal Sub-division, Sale and Development of
      Vacant Land 1*
1.2 Land Invasions and Squatting 3
1.3 Engagement with Formal Authorities 9
1.4 Incremental Development of Informal Settlements 12
*1.5 Costs and Benefits of Informal Urban Housing
      Processes 15*

**2   Public Sector Intervention in Low-Income
      Group Housing**   17

*2.1 'Conventional' Public Housing – The Public
      Works Tradition 20*
2.2 Slum Clearance 25
2.3 Organised (Aided) Self-help 28

**3   Participation, Enabling Supports and 'Non-conventional'
      Housing Strategies**   33

3.1 Participation 34
3.2 Devolution 37
*3.3 Enabling Supports – Sites and Services and Informal
      Settlement ('Slum') Upgrading 40*
3.4 Limits of the 'Self-help' and the Participation Paradigm 48

4 Three Case Studies of Enabling Support Strategies   63

4.1 The Sri Lanka Million Houses Programme 63
4.2 Rio de Janeiro Favela Bairro Programme, Brazil 68
*4.3 Oshakati Human Settlements Improvement
    Programme, (OHSIP) Namibia 74*
4.4 Lessons from the Case Studies 79

**5 The Return to 'Conventional' Public Housing Provision
and Incentives to Private Sector Developers**   83

6 Where Next   87

6.1 City Development Strategies 89
6.2 Housing-need Sub-groups 90
6.3 Cultural Integration and Cosmopolitan Development 91
6.4 Gender Needs and Assets 92
6.5 Climate Change and Geophysical Hazards 93
6.6 Energy Conservation and Environmental Sustainability 97

7 Partnership Paradigm for the Twenty-first Century   104

7.1 The Case for Incremental Housing Strategies 105
7.2 Rental Housing 114

8 Components of Support to Incremental Development   120

8.1 Land and Location 120
8.2 Finance 127
8.3 Infrastructure and Services 129
8.4 Beneficiary Selection 132
8.5 Site Planning, Building Controls and Supports 134
8.6 Community Organisation and Asset Management 136
8.7 The Private Sector 137
8.8 Strategic Planning 140

**9 Some Conclusions, Capacity Building and the
Way Forward**   145

9.1 Capacity Building 145
9.2 In Conclusion – The Way Ahead 149

Index   152

Abbreviations and Acronyms

ACCA	Asian Coalition for Community Action
ACHR	Asian Coalition for Housing Rights
ADB	Asian Development Bank
AfDB	African Development Bank
ASH	aided self-help
AWPD	Ashaiman Women for Progressive Development, Ghana
BMA	Bangkok Metropolitan Administration, Thailand
BNH	Banco Nacional da Habitação, Brazil
BOSC	Busti Baseer Odhikar Surakha Committee, Bangladesh
CAP	community action planning
CBO	community-based organisation
CDC	Community Development Council, Sri Lanka
CDS	City Development Strategy
CIDA	Canadian International Development Agency
CHF	Cooperative Housing Foundation International
CLT	community land trust
CMC	Colombo Municipal Council
CODI	Community Organisation Development Institute, Thailand
CUP	Coalition for the Urban Poor, Bangladesh
DANIDA	Danish International Development Agency
DFID	Department for International Development, United Kingdom
DM	district manager
EIA	International Energy Agency
FSDVM	Fundación Salvadoreña de Desarollo y Vivienda Minima, El Salvador
FLISP	Finance Linked Individual Subsidy Programme, South Africa
GIS	geographic information system
GIZ	Gesellschaft für Internationale Zusammenarbeit
HDA	Hyderabad Development Authority
HDD	Housing Development Department, Nairobi

HIC	Habitat International Coalition
HOLP	Housing Options and Loans Package, Sri Lanka
HUDCO	Housing and Urban Development Corporation, India
ICT	Instituto de Crédito Territorial, Colombia
IDB	Inter-American Development Bank
IDP	internally displaced person
IDRC	International Development Research Centre, Canada
IIED	International Institute for Environment and Development
IRDP	Integrated Residential Development Programme, South Africa
IYSH	United Nations International Year of Shelter for the Homeless, 1987
LAC	Latin America and the Caribbean
LISP	Low Income Settlements Programme, Guyana
MENA	Middle East and North Africa
MHP	Sri Lanka Million Houses Programme
MLGH	Ministry of Local Government and Housing, Namibia
MoA	Municipality of Aleppo
NCC	Nairobi City Council
NGO	non-governmental organisation
NGDO	non-governmental development organisation
NHDA	National Housing Development Authority, Sri Lanka
NSDF	National Slum Dwellers Federation, India
OHLM	Office d'Habitat de Loyers Moderes
OHSIP	Oshakati Human Settlements Improvement Programme, Namibia
OTC	Oshakati Town Council
PCC	Colombian Communist Party
PfA	Platform for Action
PLHP	Public Low-Cost Housing Program, Malaysia
PPP	public-private partnership
SAP	structural adjustment programme
SDG	Sustainable Development Goal
SDI	Shack/Slum Dwellers International
SIDA	Swedish International Development Cooperation Agency
SMA	Municipal Housing Department, Rio de Janeiro
SPARC	Society for the Promotion of Area Resource Centres
S&S	sites and services
SSD	Slum and Shanty Division, Sri Lanka
TDR	transferable development rights
UDA	Urban Development Authority, Sri Lanka

UNCED	United Nations Conference on Environment and Development
UN-Habitat	United Nations Human Settlements Programme
UNHCR	United Nations High Commission for Refugees
UNICEF	United Nations Children's Fund
UNDP	United Nations Development Programme
USAID	United States Agency for International Development
WCED	World Commission on Environment and Development

Foreword

By John F.C. Turner

Patrick Wakely's book has helped me greatly to see the three key issues raised by searching for patterns in placemaking. Especially useful is his account of the three international Habitat conferences: in Vancouver, 1976; Istanbul, 1996; and Quito, 2016; all were focused on the relationships between urban housing policies and urban settlement by people, especially in newly and recently modernising countries with low to negligible per capita tax bases. From the NGO Habitat Forum in 1975 the difference between the languages of governmental policies and of non-governmental initiatives has been all too clear.

This first, deepest and most challenging issue is evident in the conflicting attitudes and values discussed in Pat's detailed attention to incremental development, the oldest way of achieving stable towns, cities and their regions – and implicitly to the megacity challenge of post-capitalism that will have to cope with the inevitable consequences of climate and demographic changes. The following and more tractable questions arise in the ways and means in which placemaking is carried out, by whom and how. Pat's unanswerable case for incremental development is based on the fact that, given adequate access to land, basic resources and freedom to control key local development decisions within rational limits, people and their local organisations can and often do build and maintain attractive places serving wide ranges of individual priorities in community-building ways.

My wife and I have been living in a classic 'incremental development': St. Mary's Terrace, Hastings, East Sussex since 1989. One of a sub-terrace of four, ours was built in 1841, well before it had piped water and drainage. Along with many other sub-terraces, an almost continuous terrace of 75 dwellings was built between 1825 and 1875. It is now a fully up-dated, beautiful, friendly and probably most highly sought-after road in the town.

Pat persuasively argues that the potentials for the variety, economy and community-building that incremental development can provide, depend on the principle of subsidiarity – raising the issue of power and capacity. Significantly, despite common usage, the Oxford English Dictionary (OED) defines power as capacity first and secondly as power over others, whether they have the capacity or not. The case studies of incremental development in Pat's book highlight the incapacity of large supra-local organisations to carry out incremental, local community-led development and therefore to meet the 'requisite demands' for variety. As W.R. Ashby's law states 'If stability (of a complex system) is to be attained, the variety of the controlling system must be at least as great as the variety of the system to be controlled'. The corollary, suggested by my friend Mike Franks, makes the dependency of requisite variety on subsidiarity even more clearly: 'any organisation seeking management control over a complex system inevitably reduces its diversity to below that of the organisation itself'.

It follows that true economy and therefore social justice, also depend on subsidiarity as the full statement declares: 'It's an injustice and at the same time a grave evil and disturbance of right order to assign to a greater and higher association what lesser and subordinate organisations can do. For every social activity ought of its very nature to furnish help to the members of the body social and never destroy and absorb them'.

However difficult it may be to observe, let alone calculate the assessment of the variety of people's dwelling priorities unless 'needs' are understood as priorities for the essentials of an inhabitable dwelling: an accessible location, an acceptable duration of tenure and enough shelter and privacy – as distinct from meaningless 'needs' or wants that misstate 'housing problems', simplistically assumed to be a vital priority for a dwelling of minimally acceptable standards irrespective of individual or households' situations.

The complementary issue that also demands more attention is the appalling misuse and therefore misunderstanding of 'economy' as a synonym for money. As Vendana Shiva points out, resources are the material means of making economic use of what should be regarded as a 'commons' that, in earlier times, and still occasionally, referred to as 'God given' and plentifully available as it is self-renewing: earth and rock, water and air, sunlight and wind. But they can be polluted through abuse, such as using compound interest to make money instead of useful things. Pollute is clearly defined in the OED as the defilement of persons, the dirtying of the environment and the desecration of life. The opposite, surely our criteria for thought and action, is the triple meaning of: community as group-based personal relationships; societies built of such communities; and awareness of, and respect for, the web of life on which we all depend.

The issue for assessing right and wrong raised by these criteria is underlined by the ways in which we understand and learn from experience; feedback from consequences from what has been done; and the often ignored, feedforward loop from the hopes and fears, values and beliefs that motivate and drive our responses to situations or events that demand action and require imagination and foresight – a matter of language and translations of vocabularies as I mention above.

Preface

Housing constitutes some 60–80 per cent of the developed land of urban areas and in the order of 50–70 per cent of the value of the fixed capital formation of towns and cities (UN-Habitat 2003). Thus the production, maintenance and management of housing play fundamental roles in developing cities.[1]

Urban housing policies in the first decades of the twenty-first century are in disarray. Throughout the second half of the twentieth century there was a steady and coherent development of approaches to government intervention in the procurement of affordable and sustainable housing for the lower urban income groups in developing countries.

Globally, the history of government engagement in the provision of housing is very short – at most, only commencing since the 1950s. Prior to the mid-twentieth century, government housing production was confined to the provision of accommodation for military and some public sector civil employees, for the periods during which they were in government service in a particular locality. The procurement of housing for the vast majority of the population was seen as the responsibility of individual households in a private sector market.

Housing production was clearly regarded as an architectural and engineering function of the building and civil engineering industries. So for civil servants, housing production was the responsibility, and a minor activity, of departments or ministries of public works. Its management was confined to routine maintenance and the administration of allocation procedures. Governments' intervention in the housing provision of the vast majority of citizens was confined to attempts to control private sector initiative in the interests of public health, safety and amenity by imposing statutory standards, through the administration of development control legislation and planning and building regulations that most low-income households could not afford to meet, and many city governments were unable to enforce.

In addition, in several countries, attempts were made to increase the supply of housing affordable to lower income groups and limit the extent of exploitation by private sector landlords, by the imposition of rent controls on urban property. However in many cases, rent controls rendered the supply and maintenance of urban housing commercially uneconomic, leading to its abandonment and/or deterioration. In some South Asian countries governments attempted to impose a limit on the number of urban properties that any private sector landlord was allowed to own.

As a consequence of increasing urban homelessness and the growth of slums, from the 1950s governments throughout the world started to intervene more directly in the procurement of urban housing by establishing housing authorities (quangos), departments or ministries or extending the mandates of ministries of public works to embrace the formulation and implementation of new policies and strategies for the production of dwellings at (subsidised) prices that would be affordable to households in the lower-income groups. Over time the political and operational bases for public housing developed and took on wider objectives than simply the production of residential accommodation. Thus, the second half of the twentieth century was characterised by the design, development, testing and institutionalising of alternative strategies for public sector intervention in the production, maintenance and management of urban housing, explicitly engaging in the wider issues of social development of which the construction of dwellings and management of environmental infrastructure were but components.

These strategies were characterised by the provision of supports to enable urban households and communities to participate in the planning, development and management of their own domestic environments. Participatory 'enabling' policies were promoted by the 'Istanbul Declaration' and 'The Habitat Agenda' that emanated from the United Nations Conference on Human Settlements (Habitat II) in Istanbul in 1996. However, in the early years of the twenty-first century many governments started to abandon this process in which the procurement of dwellings was a significant by-product of, and in some instances a vehicle for, fostering social mobility and the integration of low-income communities into mainstream urban societies, economies and environmental conditions.

This, the third public policy shift, centred on a seeming return to 'conventional' housing procurement by providing incentives (regulatory concessions and financial subsidies) to private sector capitalist developers to construct dwellings for low-income group households, thereby denying households and communities the limited role that they had had in determining the development of their own domestic environments.

In response, The Quito Declaration on Sustainable Cities and Human Settlements for All and The New Urban Agenda,[2] endorsed by 167 national governments at the United Nations Conference on Housing and Sustainable Urban Development (Habitat III) in Quito in 2016, called for a return to more people-centred social and participatory approaches to urban development. It lays out 175 'politically correct' principles for housing and urban policy, couched in somewhat platitudinous 'international-UN-speak'. Although the last 50 clauses of the New Agenda fall under the heading 'Means of Implementation', no tangible indications are given for practical action, or how and by whom, it should be implemented (UN-Habitat 2016).

This book sets out to assist the search for new, and renewed, approaches to urban housing policies and strategies for their implementation by reexamining and drawing lessons from past experiences of planning and managing urban housing, particularly that of lower income group households and communities, and suggesting strategic approaches to the way ahead. Drawing on alternative paradigms and theoretical concepts, and my own experience over some four decades, emphasis is given to operational strategies for public sector engagement in urban housing delivery, maintenance and management, based on the principle of subsidiarity and authentic, risk- and benefit-sharing partnerships with low-income group households and communities.

Notes

1 'Developing' in the title of this book is used as the present participle (gerund) of the <u>verb</u> 'to develop' rather than as an adjective that qualifies the majority of towns and cities in the Global South, though this interpretation is also pertinent.
2 The UN-Haitat New Urban Agenda is supported by the United Nations Sustainable Development Goals (SDGs) 2015–2030, adopted by the UN General Assembly in September 2015; of particular relevance is Goal 11: 'to make cities and human settlements inclusive, safe, resilient and sustainable'.

References

UN-Habitat, 2003, *The Challenge of Slums: Global Report on Human Settlements 2003*, (revised 2010), Earthscan, London, UK.
UN-Habitat, 2016, *Habitat III New Urban Agenda*. Online at: http://habitat3.org/wp-content/uploads/N1639668-English.pdf

Acknowledgements

I owe gratitude to The Cities Alliance, specially Billy Cobbett and Julian Baskin, and The Development Planning Unit (DPU), University College London, specially Julio Dávila and Caren Levy, who gave me the opportunity to produce working papers in which I developed the first part (Chapters 1–5)[1] and last part (Chapters 6–9)[2] of the book. I am indebted to Elizabeth Riley, who co-authored the Cities Alliance working paper with me and with whom I researched and wrote *Communities and Communication: Building Urban Partnerships.*[3]

David Satterthwaite, Ronaldo Ramirez, Babar Mumtaz, Jorge Fiori, Caroline Moser, Michael Safier and Farouk Tebbal each gave me invaluable encouragement and advice on early drafts or parts of the book, for which I am very grateful, as I am to John Turner, who also wrote the Foreword.

Patrick Wakely
London, May 2017

Notes

1 Wakely, P., 2014, *Urban Public Housing Strategies in Developing Countries: Whence and Whither Paradigms, Policies, Programmes and Projects*, DPU60 Working Paper 'Reflections' series, No. 163/60, UCL, London, UK. An edited version of which was also published as: Wakely, P., 2016, 'Reflections on public housing paradigms, policies, programmes and projects in developing countries', *International Journal of Urban Sustainable Development*, Vol. 8. No. 1, Taylor and Francis, Abingdon, UK.
2 Wakely, P. & E. Riley, 2011, *The Case for Incremental Housing*, Cities Alliance Policy Research and Working Paper Series, No. 1, The Cities Alliance, Washington DC, USA.
3 Riley, E. & P. Wakely 2005, *Communities and Communication: Building Urban Partnerships*, ITDG Publishing, Rugby, UK.

1   Informal Housing Procurement Processes

Before launching on an examination of alternative approaches to state interventions in urban housing markets on behalf of the lowest income groups, it is useful to briefly review the strategic mechanisms by which low-income urban households and communities house themselves informally, using their own resources. These approaches are generally regarded as illegal and have been actively resisted and obstructed by governments – the police and on occasions in some countries, the military. Broadly, there are two basic approaches to the informal development of land and property. These are outlined in the sections below.

1.1 The Informal Sub-division, Sale and Development of Vacant Land

This generally occurs on the peri-urban fringes of cities and varies widely with the topographical, economic and political characteristics of different geographies and societies. A universally common occurrence is the unauthorised subdivision and sale of peri-urban agricultural or vacant land by its owners when they recognise that higher financial returns can be made by selling small plots for development, even at prices that are affordable to low-income households, than from agricultural production, grazing or quarrying, etc.

Land made available for housing in this way is made affordable to the lowest income groups by the risk-cost imposed by its illegality. Even though the purchasers have paid for it 'in good faith' and often have officially endorsed receipts to prove transaction, its sub-division into housing plots and building on it are formally considered illegal for one, or several of a variety of reasons, such as:

Figure 1.1 Caracas, Venezuela, (2005): Informal street names allocated by the landowner or informal (middle-man) developer to give 'address identity' before informal sale of plots. (Photo: Julio Dávila)

- the transfer of ownership has not been legally registered;
- its development for housing is in contravention of official master plan land use zoning;
- plot sizes and building construction are not in accordance with planning and building regulations;

any of which may carry the threat of official confiscation of land and/or demolition of buildings.

A large part of the extraordinary growth of Bogotá, Colombia in the 1950s and 1960s was due to the proliferation of *barrios piratas* as farmers and other landowners sub-divided and sold their land on the city's fringes to informal developers and speculators (Valenzuela & Vernez 1974). Similar processes have been common in cities of the Middle East and North Africa, particularly at times of extensive rural–urban migration and periods of drought that have reduced agricultural productivity and, therefore, the value of agricultural land and threatened the livelihoods of those employed in agriculture, forcing them to seek alternatives in urban job markets, thereby augmenting both the supply of, and demand for, low-cost urban and peri-urban property (Léna 2012).

1.2 Land Invasions and Squatting

This process, in which land is occupied and developed unilaterally without any form of negotiation, agreement or payment between the landowners and informal 'settler/developers', takes one of two forms: (1) organised collective land invasion; (2) plot-by-plot squatting by individual households,[1] notably in situations where the delivery of urban land was inefficient, often as the result of highly centralised government policies. An interesting example was Haouch Mokhfi in Algeria in the 1970s in which informal land subdivisions responded to the needs of both low-income groups as well as middleclass households, fortuitously resulting in cohesive social mixes.

Land Invasions

The mass invasion of relatively large parcels of urban land by organised groups of households under common leadership, sometimes controlled and supported by formal political organisations that also provided technical and managerial expertise to the settlement process, was common in Latin American cities in the 1950s and 1960s.

For instance in Bogotá, Colombia, on the Easter holiday weekend in April 1966 a group of some 300 homeless families (c. 1,500 people), organised and led by Colombian Communist Party (PCC) activists, invaded a large area of vacant land close to the historic centre of the city that was reserved for the extension of an important hospital. After a fierce battle with the police, the land was laid out (with corner marker-posts) into individual plots with a regular grid of streets, with PCC technical assistance. Each plot was then allocated to an invader family who rapidly put up temporary shelters of scrap materials and some tents in order to claim their squatter's residential rights and the area was declared a city *barrio* (neighbourhood) by the invasion's leaders with the name of Policarpa, in honour of Policarpa Salavarrieta, an important and popular heroine of the Colombian war of independence from Spain (1816–20). In subsequent years, the original makeshift structures were replaced by substantial permanent buildings (Figure 1.2) and urban infrastructure (water and sanitation) networks connected to every dwelling and paved streets and service buildings (primary schools, health centres, police posts, a market and other community facilities) were negotiated with the relevant city authorities by the community's leadership. So by the start of the twenty-first century, Policarpa was a permanent and formally recognised part of the city's fabric, society and economy (Figure 1.3), known and patronised citywide as a centre for the retail of furnishing and clothing textiles.

Figure 1.2 Barrio Policarpa, Bogotá, Colombia, 1976: ten years after the invasion and settlement of the land in 1966. (Photo: Patrick Wakely)

Figure 1.3 Barrio Policarpa, Bogotá, Colombia, 2016: fifty years after the invasion and settlement of the land in 1966. (Photo: Luz Stella Echeverri)

Squatting by Accretion

The accretion or the gradual take-over of land, plot by plot, was the process by which individual households gradually built up sizable squatter settlements plot by plot. The extensive and highly visible *ranchos* on the steep sloping mountainsides that surround the centre of Caracas, Venezuela, clearly illustrate the process of informal settlement development by accretion and the incremental process by which they were consolidated by their occupants (Figure 1.4). Another, well-known example is the Mathare Valley, close to the city centre of Nairobi, Kenya, that developed over time as a series of squatter 'villages' of increasing density and dangerously unsanitary environmental conditions, stretching to the east of the city (Figure 1.5).

Either of these processes may take place on peri-urban vacant land or on inner-city empty plots or on undeveloped land destined for public or private use, or that has not been built upon because it is geologically unstable, such as steep slopes or land that is liable to inundation, or that is being retained as open space, for a particular functional reason, such as railway or water course reservations, or that is awaiting development by either the public or private sector. Clearly informal settlements on such sites can subject their occupants to considerable danger (Hardoy & Satterthwaite 1989).

Figure 1.4 Caracas, Venezuela, (1972): The first-comer settlers were able to occupy land at the foot of the mountain, close to the city centre infrastructure networks, to which they connected informally. As land on the lower slopes became fully occupied, later-comers had to construct their dwellings further up the mountainside with more difficult access and no infrastructure services, for which they had to descend to the valley below. (Photo: Patrick Wakely)

Figure 1.5 Huruma, Nairobi, Kenya, (2004): The settlement, on publicly-owned land at the East end of Mathare Valley, grew by accretion and infill since its first settlement by squatters, evicted from other informal settlements in the city, in 1977, so that by 2000 it had a density of more than 600 dwellings per hectare (c.1,625 people /ha) and virtually no public or private open space, even for access pathways. (Photo: Patrick Wakely)

Figure 1.6 Colombo, Sri Lanka, (2006). Informal housing on a canal bank reservation (land officially kept clear of obstruction to facilitate canal maintenance operations). (Photo: Patrick Wakely)

Organised land invasions and the resulting 'squatter' settlements have tended to be on the fringes of towns and cities, where relatively large parcels of undeveloped land are available.[2] Many low-income households, however, cannot afford to be located at distances far from centres of casual employment or

Figure 1.7 Kolkata, India (1972). Permanent pavement squatters.
(Photo: Patrick Wakely)

Figure 1.8 Ahmedabad, India (1972). Informal development on public sidewalk
pavement. Occupants supply milk to neighbourhood upper-income
households – cattle and buffalos kept behind dwellings.
(Photo: Patrick Wakely)

outlets for low-skilled enterprise and therefore depend on securing affordable accommodation in city-centre locations, such as are provided by abandoned buildings or squatting on road reservations, street sidewalks and pavements.

In many cities, the demand, very often by the poorest of the urban poor, for city-centre accommodation, has led to an informal market in high-density, and very often high-rise, shelter provision that typically is let at extortionate prices. In towns and cities that have a sizable stock of abandoned or under-used buildings these are unofficially let by their owners or squatted by informal real estate entrepreneurs who rent or sell rooms to poor households. This is particularly common in the older cities of South and East Asia and the Middle East and North Africa. It has also led to the informal/illegal construction of multi-storey blocks of small apartments and single rooms, often of dangerously low standards of construction that are rented to poor households. Such informal speculative development is often built on the sites of demolished low-density, former upper-income group residential properties or land that has not been developed because it is geologically unstable (Simms 2010; Wakely & Abdul-Wahab 2010).

Figure 1.9 Tal al Zarazier, Aleppo, Syria, (2008). High-density informal development on a disused un-stabilised open garbage dump, close to the city centre, with a subterranean stream running through it. Subsequent informal construction on roofs added to the frequent collapse of entire buildings, causing injury and loss of life. (Photo: Patrick Wakely)

1.3 Engagement with Formal Authorities

As indicated in the sections above, eventually the occupants of informal settlements have to negotiate and collaborate with the formal urban authorities or political decision-makers in order to gain a level of security to their property and to access urban infrastructure and services. Towards the end of the 1980s, there was increasing evidence of semi-formal collaboration between squatter communities and municipal authorities and/or local politicians, thereby establishing processes of 'co-production' of housing (Mitlin 2008), the characteristics of which often tended to be more 'informal' than 'formal' (see Case Study 1).

The pragmatic need to gain access to urban infrastructure and services and to enhance security of tenure to land and property ultimately led to closer, more consolidated collaborative engagement between informal communities and government authorities in 'slum' upgrading programmes, discussed in Chapter 3, and, further on, to the production, maintenance and management of low-income group urban housing by authentic stakeholder partnerships embracing organised community groups, local governments and administrations and engaged private sector enterprises, as discussed in Chapter 7.

Case Study 1

Informal Land Appropriation Processes in Colombo North, Sri Lanka

In the early 1990s, a new form of organised illegal land invasion developed in Colombo, replacing the previous processes whereby informal settlements grew incrementally over time as new households settled one-by-one on vacant land in proximity to other squatters, in order to secure a measure of solidarity and security in numbers. The cases below illustrate two types of 'organised' land appropriation for low-income housing, prevalent in Colombo – one through the political system, the other through informal entrepreneurial initiative. Both these processes provided land at costs that were affordable to low-income households, that was reasonably secure and to which they seem likely to be able to obtain service connections and, in the long run, freehold title. (Both were recounted in October 2007, towards the end of the Sri Lanka Civil War 1983–2009.)

(continued)

(continued)

Settlement A (as recounted by a resident in one such settlement)

Colombo North is a haven for newcomers to the city, particularly poor people from the war-torn districts of the North and East of the country. There are many Tamil and Muslim families here and it is easy to 'get lost'. It is a safe place to be. Also it is close to the port and fish and vegetable markets are close and it is relatively easy to find a job in the informal sector. But you have to have contacts before you come to Colombo – someone to look after you. You can't just put up a shanty on a piece of vacant land as in the old days. You will be questioned about connections to terrorists. And many vacant plots are being guarded and developed with high-rise buildings (meaning, two storeys – ground plus first floor).

However, if you need land to settle down in Colombo North, there are people who will help you to purchase land in communities. They are new communities. Most public lands in Colombo North are public lands which are either reservations belonging to the Port or Railway Authorities, old municipal dump sites or canals or low lands kept as flood retention areas.

What happens is that a person who has contacts with high-level politicians or a local politician puts up two or three shacks on public land. Then he brings some earth and fills the floor and asks his people to stay there for some time. If there is no objection from the government they will continue staying there. If there are objections from government, a local politician may intervene with authorities demonstrating his power and arguing that it was done by his poor constituents who had no place to live. He may get support from a high-level politician in the ruling party in order to prevent any police actions. At the same time he will use his contacts in CMC [Colombo Municipal Council] to provide some form of water supply to the land. It goes on like that for five or six months. Then the local 'land mafia' make arrangements to sell these shacks to people who really need them. People will buy such shacks at various prices and stay under the protection of local strong guys who arrange to get their names registered in the electoral roll.

Once some families have settled like that, the 'developers' put up some more huts and keep them empty for some time and sell them to any buyers. Once people have lived in those huts for more than one year they can apply for private water and electricity connections from government authorities at a subsidised price. The water and electricity authorities provide such facilities to the poor with CMC or the Grama Niladari's (grassroots-level government official) approval.

Most of the new shanties in Colombo North have been built like this over the last five to eight years. Some municipal council members have improved access roads and drains in these newly built communities with their municipal decentralised budget money.

Settlement B (as told by a community leader – a woman)

In 2004 the popular and influential local municipal councillor (MMC), took control of a well-located but low-lying parcel of marshy land close to the Kelani River (known as 219 Watte) that belonged to CMC and was used informally for growing 'greenleaf' vegetables. Using his decentralised budget allocation, the municipal councillor filled and concreted the land, installed a tap and two public toilets, and subdivided the land into 162 plots of 10' x 15' (3.3m x 6.0m). The plots were then distributed to landless households from different parts of the city. (One beneficiary got a plot because her husband had 'done some work' for a friend of the Mayor of Colombo.)

The 162 disparate families then set about constructing their houses, predominantly using second-hand timber for walls and corrugated iron and cement fibre sheets for roofs. (The Electricity Board later gave metered connections to houses that had concrete or brick party walls; the rest (majority) hijacked it from neighbours.) They also started to form a Community Development Council (CDC), which by 2007 boasted a 100 per cent household membership.

The MMC arranged for the electoral commissioner to allocate each household an electoral number and an address in the settlement (thereby increasing his vote base). A letter, signed by the heads of all 162 households, was then sent by the CDC chairperson to the minister of urban development requesting the issue of enumeration cards for each plot, to which the secretary replied saying that the request had been forwarded to the National Housing Development Authority (NHDA). At the same time, the CDC chairperson visited the Urban Development Authority (UDA) two or three times to request household connections to services.

By November 2007 it was understood that the land was in the process of being vested in the NHDA by the CMC so that enumeration cards (or entitlement certificates) could be issued. As soon as this process is in hand the CDC will start to pressure the NHDA to upgrade them to freehold title deeds.

Since 2006, some 15 plots in 219 Watte have been sold for Rs.25–30,000 (US$250–300). But households are aware that with NHDA enumeration cards they would fetch Rs.300,000–400,000 (US$3,000–4,000) and significantly more if they had freehold title.

1.4 Incremental Development of Informal Settlements

An important characteristic of informal housing development processes has been the incremental nature of house building, infrastructure installation and provision of urban services. Householders construct, extend and improve their dwellings when these become a high priority for the investment of their resources and energy and when disposable resources become available to them. Similarly, the negotiation and installation of urban infrastructure can take a long time to complete and implement. This incremental process may take several years to accomplish during which many informal settlements remain in a 'half-developed' state that typically has been aesthetically offensive to much of the formal establishment that has tended to

Figure 1.10 Barrio Policarpa, Bogotá, Colombia, (1980). The architectural
          styles and standard of construction of each floor of this house
          clearly reflect the growing fortunes and changing preferences of its
          owner over the fifteen-year period of its incremental construction.
          Right from the start, he/she built a second entrance door with the
          ambition of being able to sub-let part of the house in the future, in
          order to supplement his/her income. The neighbours on either side
          have chosen not to invest so much in their dwellings, or they have
          been unable to do so. (Photo: Patrick Wakely)

refer to them as 'slums' and vest them with, frequently unjustifiable, pejora-
tive physical and social characteristics.

Incremental procurement of urban housing is not confined to low-
income households. Almost all permanent and serviced housing is
procured as an incremental process that takes place over relatively long
periods of time. Only a minute segment of any urban society – the excep-
tionally wealthy – has the liquid monetary assets to purchase outright or
construct their dwellings as a one-off event. Upper and middle-income
households with regular incomes and collateral guarantees have access to
long-term credit – housing loans and mortgages – that may take between
15 and 30 years of incremental repayments to amortise. Households with
low or irregular incomes and no access to formally recognised collateral or
financial guarantees, construct minimal basic dwellings at very low cost,
which they extend and improve as more resources become available and
as the need for bigger or better structures becomes a priority. This process
of extension and modification can take decades, or may be never ending.

The incremental housing process not only has financial benefits that enable
low-income households to access affordable housing when and where they need
it, but it has also been important in building social capital (community cohesion and local governance and management capacities in otherwise socially
disparate new urban communities) through the incremental development of
locally controlled and managed neighbourhood infrastructure, services and
amenities as well as the construction and improvement of individual dwellings.

Figure 1.11 Antop Hill, Bombay (Mumbai), India (1973): 'Cosmopolitan Hutment
Dwellers Association'; locally organised squatter settlement on flood-
prone land. (Photo: Patrick Wakely)

Table 1.1 SWOT Analysis of Informal Urban Housing Processes

SWOT Analysis	Strengths	Weaknesses	Opportunities	Threats
for occupant households and communities	Affordable, socially acceptable Housing in sufficient quantities in acceptable locations.	No secure title and threat of eviction, causing reluctance to invest in the improvement of properties and neighbourhoods.	Formal recognition on terms that allow security of title and the impetus to invest in housing and neighbourhood development.	Inappropriate government policies that remove market advantages of informality, forcing low-income households into higher densities (overcrowding) and/or untenable locations.
for city government and administration	Low-income group housing and neighbourhoods developed at negligible capital cost to government.	Non-compliance with planning (zoning) and building standards, occasionally leading to threats to public health and safety; high infrastructure maintenance costs.	An experienced proactive resource for the management of low-income group housing procurement throughout the city; contributor to municipal revenue.	Organised crime will take a stronger hold on informal markets preventing progressive initiatives to regularise them, leading to their deterioration and increase. Low-income groups become easy prey to populist political parties.
for city society and economy	Accommodation for the city's labour force, and for down-stream (informal sector) production that feeds formal industry and commerce, at no cost to government.	Perceptions of social and environmental degradation; fear of social instability.	The valorisation of property and the development of stable lower middle-income neighbourhoods and enterprises; contributions to municipal revenue.	Lack of appropriate policies will lead to the creation of slums, the deterioration of health and education and lowering of productivity and social unrest.

1.5 Benefits and Costs of Informal Urban Housing Processes

Inevitably, there is a danger of over-simplification and stereotyping in attempting to summarise the perceived attributes of informal housing processes globally in a single SWOT table such as Table 1.1. Nevertheless, it can be observed with some confidence that the preponderance of government and city administrations has tended to give greater credence to the, often erroneous, perceptions of the 'weaknesses' and 'threats' of urban informal settlements than to their 'strengths' and possible 'opportunities', despite the fact that numerically they constituted well over half the housing stock of many cities in developing countries and increased at rates that have responded to demand in a way that formal housing production had been typically unable to achieve. In addition there is extensive and growing evidence that, even with no official support, except perhaps a little tolerance, informally procured housing developed and managed by communities of low-income households, develops over time into cohesive urban neighbourhoods, integrated into the fabric of the city, as in the case of the Policarpa neighbourhood in Bogotá, described above (see Figures 1.2 and 1.3). Another widely known and very impressive example, also in Latin America, is the invasion, settlement and development of Villa El Salvador to the south of Lima, Peru, that was started in 1970 by a group of some 80–100 rural–urban immigrant families, which by 1990 had grown into a modern formally recognised municipality within Lima District, covering some 35km^2 with a population of almost 400,000 (Peattie 1990).

Notes

1 The majority of land invasions tended to be of public land, essentially in situations where public authorities were either complacent for political reasons or corrupt.
2 Policarpa Salavarrieta in Bogotá in 1966 was exceptional in that the large area of undeveloped land, being held for the expansion of the Hospital de la Hortúa, happened to be centrally located in the city.

References

Hardoy, J. & D. Satterthwaite, 1989, *Squatter Citizen*, Earthscan, London, UK.
Léna, E., 2012, 'Mukhalafat in Damascus: The form of an informal settlement', in Ababsa, M. et al. (eds), *Popular Housing and Land Tenure in the Middle East*, The American University in Cairo Press, Cairo, Egypt and New York, USA.
Mitlin, D., 2008, 'With and Beyond the State: Co-production as a route to political influence, power and transformation for grass-roots organizations, *Environment & Urbanization*, Vol. 20, No. 2, Sage, London, UK.

Peattie, L., 1990, 'Participation: A case study of how invaders organize, negotiate and interact with government in Lima, Peru', Environment & Urbanization, Vol. 2, No. 1, London, UK.

Simms, D., 2010, *Understanding Cairo: The Logic of a City Out of Control*, The American University in Cairo Press, Cairo, Egypt.

Valenzuela, J. & G. Vernez, 1974, 'Construcción popular y estructura del mercado de vivienda: El caso de Bogotá, *Revista Interamericana de Planificación*, No. 31, Mexico.

Wakely, P. & R. Abdul-Wahab, 2010, *Informal Land and Housing Markets in Aleppo, Syria*, [English and Arabic], GIZ, Eschborn, Germany.

2 Public Sector Intervention in Low-Income Group Housing

The two decades 1950–1970 saw the political independence of many former-European colonies in Asia, Africa and the Caribbean, and the constitution of new democratic Arab republics in the Middle East and North Africa (MENA), in most cases accompanied by a rapid and significant increase in urban populations as newly independent governments encouraged the expansion of indigenous industry and commerce. In Latin America a new economic independence emerged from the extensive industrialisation that took place during the 1940s and early 1950s, which occasioned dramatic rates of urbanisation. As evidence, the 1951 and 1961 rounds of national censuses revealed the extent to which informal settlements had grown in and around towns and cities throughout the developing world. As a consequence of political pressure for action to address increasing urban homelessness and the growth of slums, governments throughout the world started to intervene more directly in the procurement of urban housing by establishing housing authorities, departments and ministries or extending the mandates of ministries of works to embrace the formulation and implementation of new policies and strategies for the production of dwellings.[1]

For instance, in India the majority of states set up state housing boards in the early 1960s to provide public housing for low- and lower-middle income groups in urban areas and in 1972 the government of India established the Housing and Urban Development Corporation (HUDCO) as a 'second tier' national housing bank to support them financially. In Indonesia the National Housing Corporation (Perumnas) and the National Housing Policy Board and Mortgage Bank were constituted in 1974. In the same year, the Thailand National Housing Authority was established as a consolidated public housing agency by merging the Welfare Housing Office of the national Public Welfare Department and the Slum Improvement (clearance) Office of Bangkok Metropolitan Administration (BMA).

Many Latin American countries also launched their first public housing policies and agencies that comprised the public provision of housing finance, the development of land and/or the construction of dwellings for rent or sale. Ministries of housing and government housing departments and agencies were established for the purpose. The Brazilian Banco Nacional da Habitação (BNH) was established in 1964 and operated successfully as a federal public housing agency and 'second-tier' lender until 1986. The Colombian Instituto de Crédito Territorial (ICT), that had been established as early as 1939 as a national housing authority, embarked on a highly productive nationwide programme of subsidised housing production for urban low- and low-middle income groups that it maintained for the following 40 years.

Mexico and Chile took a somewhat different approach, concentrating on providing legislative and financial supports and incentives to real estate developers to construct housing for the lowest income groups with the intention of enabling them to join the formal private sector urban housing market.

African governments started to intervene in urban housing markets soon after their political independence from colonialism in the late 1950s and 1960s, though generally not on the same ambitious scale as their Asian and Latin American counterparts. For instance, in 1964 the first independent government of Kenya created a national Ministry of Lands and Settlement, though the procurement of subsidised urban housing was made the responsibility of municipal government in the major cities. Similarly, in Nigeria the clearance of slums and delivery of public housing was made the responsibility of local government or local-level parastatal development authorities, such as the ambitious Lagos Executive Development Board, made famous by its slum clearance programmes and development of new dormitory towns, such as Surulere to the west of central Lagos (Marris 1961).

The subsequent history of direct public sector involvement in urban housing has been that of the initiation of ambitious public housing programmes for low-income groups, followed by the gradual withdrawal of government agencies from the direct construction of public housing. This process of apparent retreat was occasioned not only by governments' inability to meet their construction targets, but it was also in response to changes in the understanding of the role of housing in urban social and economic development. It can be characterised more positively as a four-stage sequence of increasing involvement of individual households and communities in the production of officially recognised housing, leading eventually to the '*enablement*' paradigm of support-based collaboration between central and local government, communities and individual households.

At the risk of gross over-simplification, this sequence can be broadly identified with the last four decades of the twentieth century thus:

1960s: The public works tradition of 'conventional' government-built housing and slum clearance programmes that, in the sequential model presented here, is most readily identified in Asia, Africa and the Caribbean with the post-independence period of the 1960s and in the same decade in Latin America with the dramatic urbanisation in the wake of extensive economic growth of the 1940s and 1950s.

1970s: The organised (or aided) self-help movement that was strongly promoted in the late 1960s and early 1970s, principally in Latin America.

1980s: Sites and services (S&S) projects and slum upgrading programmes that got under way in the 1970s and continued throughout the 1980s in most parts of the developing world.

1990s: Support-based policies and programmes empowering and enabling local government administrations, urban low-income communities and households to collaborate in the 'co-production' of affordable urban housing.

The more detailed historical review of these broad stages of policy development that follows is in order because of the lessons for the future that can be drawn from it. It should be remembered, however, that all stages do not fall neatly into the decades that they typify. They overlap, and even as recently as the 2000s, each approach was still employed in different countries of the developing world. Thus, although the passages that follow are written in the past tense as though the strategies they describe form a sequence that is now behind us, they are all in fact, in one form or another, a part of current policy in some countries in the second decade of the twenty-first century.[2]

Before beginning the review of the development of urban housing policies and implementation strategies, it is important to realise that prior to these policies, governments of virtually all political colours regarded the production of housing for ordinary people not in government employment or custody as the responsibility of individual households and/or private sector real estate developers and landlords.

Housing procurement activities were influenced indirectly by government through programmes that regulated them in some way or other through development control legislation on urban land approved for residential use. The most common forms of such intervention were and, in many countries, still are:

- Land use zoning and development controls to secure orderly and compatible land use and to control the environmental quality of different areas of cities, usually expressed as an urban land use master plan and accompanying legislative statutes;
- Property taxation policies to generate local public revenue on the basis of notional differentials in the distribution and consumption of urban services;

- Rent control legislation to fix a ceiling on rents charged by private sector landlords, intended to assist low-income households in finding affordable accommodation in otherwise exploitative commercial rental housing markets;
- Controls on the extent of individual property holding in urban areas in order both to redistribute the holdings of large urban property owners to their low-income tenants and to reduce the extent to which land-lords could profit from exploiting the demand for housing by the lower income groups. This measure was confined to some South Asian coun-tries (India, Bangladesh, Nepal and Sri Lanka).

Inevitably, the impact of such measures on the housing that was built, par-ticularly by the lowest income groups, was determined by the extent to which local authorities were able to enforce them. While in upper-income urban areas, land use regulations and building controls were relatively easy to enforce, this was not the case in the large and growing low-income neigh-bourhoods where such public controls were virtually impossible to police. Such was the regulatory framework in most countries in Asia, Africa, MENA and Latin America and the Caribbean (LAC) at the beginning of the 1960s.

Bearing in mind the caveats already expressed, subsequent government intervention in the procurement of low-income group housing broadly fol-lowed the four-stage trajectory alluded to above and discussed in greater detail below and in Chapter 3.

2.1 'Conventional' Public Housing – The Public Works Tradition

The first stage, often referred to as 'conventional' housing policies, stemmed from the political need for governments to be seen to intervene in the housing market in support of the lowest income groups. It was also due to a genuine concern for the orderly physical growth of cities and the appearance of the urban building stock. The aesthetic homogeneity of resi-dential areas, to some extent a legacy of the post-war modern movement in architecture, became a symbol of public affluence, good health and social wellbeing and therefore political stability with which governments and city administrations wanted to be identified by their electorate and internation-ally. It was genuinely believed that governments could provide subsidised affordable housing for all but the very poorest on the model of the post-war reconstruction of European cities and public housing programmes.

Their first task was to determine and legislate on politically accepta-ble levels of subsidy[3] to be devoted to urban housing and to set or adapt standards of space and construction that defined a 'minimum standard dwelling' and other such norms, for example concerning acceptable levels of infrastructure, service and amenity provision, that were deemed necessary and acceptable by the political managers and professional/technical staff of the new national housing agencies. So the standards of space and domestic environmental quality, although reduced, tended to be more suitable for middle-class steady-income earners than most of the urban poor. The standards became statutory norms for the production of new housing against which the existing urban housing stock could be measured in order to establish the extent to which it needed replacing.

The outcome of this exercise, together with estimates of the existing residential overcrowding, constituted a notional 'housing deficit' which, when added to projections of future population growth and the formation of new households, provided an arithmetical figure of 'housing need'. To this calculation was applied an estimate of the number of those existing and future households that could not afford even the 'minimum standard dwelling' at prevailing market prices, typically a very large proportion. This became the basis on which targets were set for the production of subsidised dwellings by the government for the lowest income groups. Such targets were rarely achieved. For example, in 1972, the Tamil Nadu state government in India set a target to eradicate all slums in Madras (Chennai) and rehouse their occupants by 1977. Over the following five years, the newly constituted Tamil Nadu Slum Clearance Board built 17,450 dwelling units. However, despite this impressive achievement around 190,000 households (almost one million people) remained in unserviced shanties in the city. Also in 1972, the Karachi Development Authority in Pakistan set a target to construct 3,040 apartments in the Jacob Lines Project to rehouse slum dwellers. By 1980, when the project was abandoned, only some 800 units had been completed. Similar examples from this period can be drawn from East Asia, Latin America and MENA.

Such public housing programmes were typified by tenement blocks of minimal-sized apartments or individual single-storey dwellings, both types were typically of relatively high-standard permanent construction with individual utility connections. They were commonly located on the urban periphery where land was available and cheap, but were therefore far from centres of employment and social amenities and with only tenuous and costly transport links. They were designed by government architects and engineers whose aim was to produce the lowest cost structures that could meet both the standards set by the by-laws and the professionals' view of 'how the urban poor should live'. In many cases, in order to minimise costs, little or no provision was made for social or community facilities or amenities.

Figure 2.1 Bandra East, Bombay (Mumbai), India, (1972). Maharashtra Housing
         Board apartments for lowest-income groups, with no allowance for public
         or community service or amenity buildings. (Photo: Patrick Wakely)

Figure 2.2 Rangoon (Yangon), Burma (Myanmar), (1972). Burma Construction
         Corporation subsidised housing on the city fringes (using precast
         concrete structural frame with low-quality brick infill construction).
         (Photo: Patrick Wakely)

There was rarely any attempt to study the particular needs of the intended
users, let alone to consult them. The beneficiaries, who were officially
qualified by having incomes below an established ceiling or who had been

displaced by slum clearance programmes, had no part in the decision-making that determined the location, design, standard of construction and level of service provision or the management of their housing.[4] There was therefore little chance that it could respond to the individual needs, demands or aspirations of any of its occupants, and no chance that it could respond to those of all of them.

Figure 2.3 George Town, Penang, Malaysia, (1972). 'Rifle Range' housing project (3,700 1- and 2-room apartments = 17,000 people on five hectares of land developed by the Ministry of Housing and Local Government, using a French precast concrete structural panel system of construction. (Photo: Patrick Wakely)

Figure 2.4 George Town, Penang, Malaysia, (1972). Fishermen and Lightermen's settlement in central George Town Harbour, re-settled by Ministry of Housing and Local Government slum clearance programme in the Rifle range project (see Fig.2.3), some families on 17th or 18th floors, with no access to the sea or their boats (their livelihoods). (Photo: Patrick Wakely)

Official controls very often extended to the use of the dwellings themselves, for example prohibiting the keeping of animals or undertaking market gardening; using the premises for commercial activity or sub-letting any part of the property; and prohibiting any extensions or modifications to the building. These arbitrary restrictions were placed upon households who were invariably dependent on being able to supplement small and irregular incomes through such activities, not only in order to feed and clothe themselves, but also to pay for their housing, whether it was allocated by hire-purchase of an eventual freehold or rented on leasehold. Despite the subsidies that were built into the housing costs, many occupants could not afford the rent or loan repayments, even though the housing was supposedly designed to meet their level of affordability.

A major consequence of this was that many housing units were sold or transferred by their intended beneficiaries to wealthier households for whom permanent accommodation had a higher priority, either as a home or as a capital, or income-earning, investment. The official reaction to this perfectly rational behaviour was frequently one of 'moral outrage' couched in terms of the 'ungrateful and mercenary' response of the urban poor in using public subsidies ('government charity') with which to speculate. Rarely was it understood or accepted that for low-income households living close to the breadline, responsibility for the maintenance and management of real estate was often low on a family's list of livelihood priorities for survival, particularly when a subsidised dwelling represented a valuable market asset to exchange either for a lump sum or an income from renting it out.

In situations where resale, transfer or subletting were not common, usually in rental housing estates which had been cheaply built to save capital costs, environmental conditions tended to deteriorate very rapidly. To a large extent, this stemmed from the occupants' exclusion from any direct involvement in the design of their dwellings, and the consequent perception that they had no responsibility for the maintenance and management of their homes and the communal spaces around them. This responsibility was considered to rest with the landlord: the housing authority. However, many public housing agencies were unable to fulfil their management and maintenance functions owing to a shortage of resources. Thus, new high-cost slums were created very rapidly. For example, many of the tenement blocks newly built by the Tamil Nadu Slum Clearance Board in the 1970s deteriorated through lack of maintenance to the extent that they were already officially re-classified as 'slums' in the late 1980s, only a decade after their construction, and together with more 'traditional' slums and shanties, they were high on the priority list for demolition or 'slum upgrading' by the Slum Clearance Board itself.

2.2 Slum Clearance

A different aspect of low-income housing policies, initiated in the 1950s and 1960s, was slum clearance. Although it often went hand-in-hand with (was followed by) the construction of new low-income group housing, slum clearance achieved its own rationale when governments saw it as their responsibility to rid cities of the 'unhealthy' and 'unsightly' slums and shanty settlements (sic) that were springing up at an ever-increasing rate. Slum clearance programmes usually concentrated on the removal of self-built shanties, rather than dealing with overcrowded, run-down central area slums in old buildings which presented much more difficult problems involving complicated ownership networks and issues of design and construction in or close to city centre business districts. A notable exception was Bombay (Mumbai), India, which in 1970 set up a Buildings Repairs and Renewal Board to give another 20 years of safe use to residential tenement buildings (chawls) in imminent danger of collapse (see Section 3.3).

In general however, slum clearance programmes solved few problems. They effectively depleted a large proportion of the urban housing stock and destabilised and alienated some of the most vulnerable communities engaged in urban development. Accounts involving the destruction of hundreds of thousands of modest but affordable urban dwellings across the

Figure 2.5 Bombay (Mumbai), India, (1973). Typical central area Chawl
buildings, built in the 1880s. (Photo: Patrick Wakely)

developing world abound. For example, in Manila, Philippines, 90,000 people were evicted and their dwellings demolished in a single three-month
period in 1964 because their homes were not considered appropriate to a
modern city by a class of urban political administrators – self-appointed
arbiters of how the urban poor should not live. In 1975–1977 more than
150,000 people lost their dwellings and many of their possessions in Delhi,
India, as part of an extensive 'city beautification' programme.

   Despite ambitious intentions to rehouse slum clearance victims in new
public housing, as in Madras (Chennai), India, referred to above, very few
were actually rehoused. Those that were, were often moved to new sites on the
urban fringes or beyond, where land was cheap and they were 'out of sight'.

Figure 2.6 Phnom Penh, Cambodia, (2001). Communities evicted from
informal neighbourhoods in the city centre and forcibly removed
to sites outside the city with no infrastructure or services (water
delivered by private vendors), where they had to start developing
a new settlement, far from centres of employment or social or
welfare facilities. (Photo: Patrick Wakely)

Such locations were invariably far from centres of employment offering
work suitable for semi-skilled and unskilled people who then had to spend
a large proportion of their low and usually unstable incomes on transport to
locations where there was access to casual or other employment opportunities. In addition, such new low-income housing areas, typically populated
by young and migrant populations, were often underserved with basic health
and educational facilities. Thus, slum clearance tended to be merely slum
relocation, as households were forced to start the painful and alienating
process of once again of setting up their homes in a different place, while
waiting for the next round of slum clearance to catch up with them. There
were, however, occasional reversals of these programmes where communities were sufficiently well organised or assisted (by supportive NGOs) to be
able to resist them.

At a different level, public housing projects put a major strain on the construction and building materials industries that were already under pressure
from other national and urban development efforts. This was aggravated by
the perception that investment in subsidised housing for the lowest income
groups was not economically productive. At best it was classified as a politically necessary 'social overhead'. Even in socialist and mixed-economy
countries, housing was not treated as a basic welfare function of the state, as
was provision for health care and education. There was, therefore, constant

political pressure to reduce the costs of public housing programmes or to curtail them in order to release government resources to the more overtly productive branches of the construction sector such as civil and agricultural engineering, transport and industrial development.

There were two common responses to such pressure. These were either to reduce the subsidies or to cut the costs, or both. The reduction of subsidies meant recovering a greater proportion, if not all, of project costs from the beneficiaries. But this, in turn, meant accepting higher income groups as beneficiaries, effectively excluding the lowest income target groups from public housing projects. For example, in 1988, the Indian HUDCO merged the two lowest income categories in its classification system for loan eligibility,[5] thereby effectively releasing state housing boards and development authorities from having to construct housing for the poorest group, who were thereby excluded from access to any public (decent) housing.

Cutting costs meant either reducing space and construction standards to below those previously set and politically accepted as 'minimum', or reducing the cost of construction. This gave rise to extensive quests to find cheaper acceptable building materials and research into the most economic planning and design techniques for low-cost housing by local, regional and international planning and building research organisations.[6] The aim to reduce the cost of construction also led to attempts to minimise the cash cost of labour in low-income group house construction by transferring some (unskilled) building operations out of the wage-earning activities of conventional construction processes by engaging the beneficiaries' participation in its construction – termed 'self-help'.

2.3 Organised (Aided) Self-help

Organised self-help, usually referred to as 'aided self-help' (ASH), housing programmes and projects were initially promoted in Latin America, principally Brazil and Colombia and, to a lesser extent, in some Asian countries,[7] by the United States Alliance for Progress international aid programme, administered by the then new US Agency for International Development (USAID) of the Kennedy administration in the early 1960s.

The principal objective of ASH was to reduce the cost of construction by engaging the future occupants in the building process as unpaid labour, often referred to at the time as 'sweat-equity' and to develop senses of 'community', 'identity', 'ownership' and 'pride' in the new residential neighbourhoods that they were about to construct, in the expectation that these sentiments would lead to good local management of community assets (local public infrastructure and services) in use after occupation of the housing and minimise the up-market selling of subsidised dwellings for a profit.

It was also hoped that as volunteer-builders, many would also gain some permanent, marketable construction industry skills that would increase their future income levels.

Project beneficiaries, who were selected on the basis of their level of income and/or other indicators of poverty and housing need, were compulsorily organised into 'work groups' that committed them to an 'agreed' input of labour over the construction period of the project. (In many projects, to ensure 'equity-of-effort' housing authority project managers went to some lengths to ensure that individuals would not be assigned to work on the houses that they would eventually be allocated and occupy.)

Case Study 2

La Presita, San Miguel, El Salvador

The ASH project, La Presita in San Miguel, El Salvador, was part of a countrywide World Bank-financed urban housing programme based on organised self-help (termed 'mutual aid', at the time). The San Miguel project began in 1974 with the plan to supply 900 housing units administered by the Fundación Salvadoreña de Desarollo y Vivienda Minima (FSDVM). The project site, La Prestina, had an innovative land development pattern in which groups of 12–15 houses were clustered around a large central semi-public open recreation area. The project had 36 such clusters in total and included a primary school, park/playground and a community centre. Beneficiary households were granted legal tenure to land, phased neighbourhood infrastructure and a core starter house, designed and built by FSDVM's contractors. Core starter options varied in design, though all had in-house water and sewerage connections and electricity. Beneficiary households were organised in 'mutual aid' work groups, each of which worked on the construction of all core houses in each cluster. Participant families were selected through a long vetting process in which each participating household agreed to provide labour to the mutual aid work groups, though some households, who met most of the conditions for selection, were deterred by being required to provide unpaid labour, which it was anticipated would entail 25–35 weekends of input. Rather than provide family labour, several households employed building labourers at below market wage rates to substitute for them. Potential beneficiaries also had to agree to not sell or rent their house for a period of five years

(continued)

(continued)

after occupation, which did not seem to be a deterrent or to have been significantly infringed.

The whole programme was evaluated by the World Bank in 1979, five years after its start, and in general was deemed to have been successful in meeting its overall objectives, though delays in the completion of projects, including the La Presita project in San Miguel, were a common failure. The principal reasons for delays were caused by the lengthy and complicated procedures for assembling land; dropouts from the mutual aid work groups causing labour shortages; and the time required to train and supervise unskilled building labourers.

There was little evidence that the programme generated any sustained increase in household incomes or provided any new marketable construction skills. The most successful projects tended to be those that rehoused families who had been evicted as whole communities from existing slums and informal urban settlements. The La Presita project in San Miguel did not produce dwellings that were significantly cheaper than conventionally constructed low-income group public housing, and householders had to pay some 48 per cent of the full cost of construction, which in many cases was made possible by gifts from the savings of family members who were not engaged in the project. This provoked the World Bank evaluators to call for a revision to the way that 'affordability' was calculated and to embrace a more complex definition of 'household wealth' than just recurrent income in any future projects.

The ASH movement was short lived as it failed to satisfy some of its basic objectives. Projects were centrally planned and managed entirely by government housing authorities; in effect they only differed from 'conventional', contractor-built public housing by the use of unpaid, theoretically voluntary, labour, which fuelled severe criticism by the programmes' detractors.

Construction costs were rarely, if ever, lower than those of the direct construction of 'conventional' housing projects as the savings gained by not paying the (unskilled) labour that was provided by project beneficiaries, who generally had no experience in even the most menial of building site tasks, significantly increased the cost of site supervision, rather than reduce it. Also the quality of the end product was invariably lower than that of 'conventional' public housing that was contractor-built by an experienced labour force. Furthermore, in most developing countries, the cost of unskilled labour represented a relatively small proportion of the total cost of building, so replacing the unskilled labour force with unpaid volunteer workers, at best, represented only a very marginal reduction in the total cost of construction.[8]

There is no evidence that the organised collective building activity ever led to better community relations than in any new neighbourhood composed of disparate urban, or migrant, households. Indeed, anecdotal accounts abound of disputes between neighbours over inequalities in the extent of labour inputs, etc., on occasions leading to serious social divisions and conflict.

The micro-management of ASH projects was complicated and cumbersome, which impacted on the macro-management of government and municipal public housing authorities and agencies. So the ASH approach was soon abandoned. Nevertheless, there are some successful examples, such as Ciudad Kennedy in Bogotá, Colombia, that, 50 years after its construction by organised self-help, was a thriving low-middle-income community and neighbourhood of high environmental quality.

The apparent inability of public housing agencies to meet targets for the construction of subsidised 'conventional' public housing, including that built by ASH, and to maintain it in use was to search for ways to reduce construction costs and to off-load responsibility for the maintenance and management of public housing. This and the extent of the proliferation of informal settlements, revealed by the 1971 round of national population censuses in virtually all cities of the developing world, called for new approaches.

Notes

1 Housing was perceived as the construction of buildings and infrastructure engineering, consequently public housing agencies and authorities tended to grow out of, or be attached to ministries or departments of public works, almost invariably at national or state government level, rather than at the level of municipal or local government.

2 An example is the case of Algeria, which in the 1960s had benefited from a huge oil revenue income during the preceding two decades. It engaged in an unprecedented urban public housing programme which benefited millions of slum dwellers and low-income groups, which was maintained. Though since the drop in oil revenue in the early 1970s, the programme's effectiveness and sustainability have been highly questionable.

3 Frequently provided as a rebate on loan interest rates and/or recovery periods; occasionally as a direct grant expressed as a percentage of the capital cost of housing production.

4 In many situations, the arbitrary relocation of slum dwellers destabilized harmonious communities, leading to hostile behaviour and civil unrest (see Section 6.3). There was also a frequent tendency to break up families as the men had to leave home to seek work elsewhere, often also joining or starting another household.

5 Economically weaker section (EWS) <Rs.350 (US$11.00) income/month and low-income group (LIG) Rs.351–600 (US$11–20) income/month. Other categories eligible for HUDCO financed housing were: middle-income group (MIG) Rs.601–1,000 (US$.20–330) income/month; and high-income group (HIG) > Rs.1,000 (US$330) income/month.

6 For example, the British government Department of Scientific and Industrial Research, Building Research Station (BRS), Overseas Division, which produced its regular series of excellent *Overseas Building Notes*; The West Africa Building Research Institute (WABRI), based in Ghana; Centro Interamericano de Vivienda y Planeamiento (CINVA or Inter-American Centre for Housing and Planning), based in Colombia; and the Indian National Building Research Organisation (NBRO), Roorkee.

7 For example, in the Philippines, where ASH was a major component of the Land for the Landless Programme in Mindoro and Palawan, and in the Indonesian Transmigration Programme in Sumatra in the 1970s. It was also the basis of the Building Together project in Bangkok, Thailand, 1979–1980, and in the Sri Lanka One Lakh Houses Programme, 1977–1982.

8 As a very rough rule-of-thumb, in European and North American countries, where construction labour costs are relatively high, the labour component of basic building, such as low-income group housing, represented c. 80 per cent and building materials and components c. 20 per cent of the total cost of construction. In most developing countries this ratio was reversed, so the cost of labour was only some 20 per cent, of which the cost of unskilled workers was but a small proportion of total labour costs.

Reference

Marris, P., 1961, *Family and Social Change in an African City*, Routledge, London, UK and New York, USA.

3 Participation, Enabling Supports and 'Non-conventional' Housing Strategies

In 1966, John F.C. Turner and Rolf Goetze, drawing on their experience of working with households and community leaders in informal neighbourhoods (*barriadas*) in Lima, Peru, brought the attention of governments and the international donor community[1] to the efficacy and productivity of informal housing processes of the urban poor, outlined in Chapter 1, making a distinction between 'slums of despair' and 'slums of hope' and persuasively arguing that, rather than being a problem and source of social deprivation and criminality most urban informal settlements 'solve more problems [of housing low-income families and communities] than they create' and that, with a change of perception, might be utilised to advantage by government housing authorities (Turner 1968).

This caught the attention of governments and the international aid donor community[2] and triggered a paradigm shift to the principle of 'subsidiarity': recognition of the need to distinguish between the roles of different actors (decision-makers and implementers) in each of the different fields and levels of the production, maintenance and management of urban housing in order to achieve optimal economic efficiency and efficacy and to devolve responsibilities to them, or to contract their services (Turner 1976). Thus, low-income households and community-based organisations (CBOs) should have key roles in all aspects of the production, maintenance and management of their dwellings and domestic infrastructure – significantly greater participation in, and responsibility for, the fundamental decisions governing their housing and local environment than in any previous public housing procurement processes.

The policy implications of this paradigm were to establish or reinforce the capacity of urban development agencies and housing authorities to initiate and manage support-based housing programmes and projects that generally embraced two components: first, the improvement or upgrading of existing sub-standard and informal settlements; and second, the development of new low-income neighbourhoods, generally through the provision of serviced land at affordable (subsidised) costs and technical, managerial and, in some programmes, (limited) financial supports for house building and neighbourhood development to individual households and CBOs.

This change in paradigm and policies, in the late 1970s, coincided with the proliferation of national and local urban non-governmental organisations (NGOs) and international non-governmental development organisations (NGDOs), most of which had their origins and bases in the developed countries of Europe and North America, with institutional interests in urban housing and other aspects of urban poverty reduction and alleviation in developing countries.

3.1 Participation

This section looks at some of the vocabulary of the participatory housing and urban development and planning paradigm that underpinned 'non-conventional' 'enabling' policies for urban housing and the concepts behind it and examines its impact on action, with emphasis on the role of government. Two fundamental issues are discussed: decentralisation and devolution.

What Is Participation?

There is an abundant literature on participation that analyses its many different interpretations and implications. Perhaps the most widely quoted is Sherry Arnstein's (1969) 'ladder of citizen participation', which identifies eight rungs on the ladder that range from 'manipulation' in a category of non-participatory communication to full 'citizen control'.[3] However for the purposes of this discussion, participation in urban development and planning may be characterised by three different interpretations that, in turn, can be seen as a progression in the international understanding of the concept of public engagement in the governance, planning and management of urban development and housing.

'Participation [Mark 1]', the first of these, may be summarised as the participation of people in governments initiated and managed programmes and projects. This, the first significant recognition of the importance of engagement of non-governmental stakeholders in public decision-making, came to the fore at the first United Nations Conference on Human Settlements in Vancouver in 1976 (Habitat I).[4] At best this level of participation embraces programmes such as 'sites and services' (S&S) in which public authorities identify land for development, draw up layout plans, install off-plot infrastructure and allocate plots for individual development by householders and enterprises within the constraints of the prevailing development control legislation. 'Participation [Mark 1]' includes the processes of public consultation in which the views of citizens and civil society organisations are sought, though with no guarantee as to the extent to which they will be heeded. 'Participation [Mark 2]' reverses this, becoming the participation of government in peoples' programmes and projects. This approach emerged during the United Nations International Year of Shelter for the Homeless (IYSH) in 1987 and the 'Global Shelter Strategy to the Year 2000' that was endorsed by the UN General Assembly in 1988. But it really hit the international stage at the United Nations Conference on Environment and Development (UNCED) – the 'Earth Summit' in Rio de Janeiro in 1992, which launched the highly influential Agenda 21 for environmental planning and management, and more importantly, Local Agenda 21 (LA21) with the slogan 'think globally and act locally'. This gave emphasis to participatory governance and the role of the state as 'enabler' to the implementation of locally made decisions. In terms of housing and urban development, emphasis shifted to urban renewal and regeneration and the upgrading of deprived environments, communities and economies on terms determined by those most involved – communities and households.

'Partnership', the third approach, in which participants share both the risks and the benefits of urban development and management, discussed at greater length in Chapter 7, came to the fore at the United Nations Conference on Human Settlements Habitat II – the 'City Summit' in Istanbul in 1996, as the principal platform for the Habitat Agenda and the UN campaigns for 'Urban Governance' and 'Security of Tenure' that followed. Partnership, characterised by the shared ownership of development initiatives, differs significantly from participation in which one party is the initiator and 'owner' of a programme or project in which the other stakeholders may participate as secondary actors. Whilst public-private partnerships (PPPs) between government and formal private sector enterprises in urban development projects were becoming increasingly common, those between government and urban low-income communities and civil society organisations are complex and real partnership has rarely been achieved. Many so-called partnerships tended to be little more than conventional subcontracting arrangements between government agencies and civil society organisations or community groups, and not authentic partnerships at all (Riley & Wakely 2005).

Not all situations lend themselves to one particular approach to participation or partnership. So, despite the historical sequence of concepts presented here, there are many conditions in which partnerships are inappropriate or, for example, in which consultation (Mark 1 Participation) is the most effective form of stakeholder collaboration. The concept of 'co-production' in which government agencies collaborate with individuals or community groups (Mitlin 2008) underpins participation [Mark 2] as presented here and is also closely identified with the formation of authentic partnerships.[5]

Urban Governance, Management and Administration

In considering different forms of participation and partnership in urban development, particularly the development of informal areas, it is important to distinguish between:

- urban *governance* as a process of decision-making and setting standards;
- the *management* of urban development – new initiatives and capital investments; and
- the routine *administration* of service delivery and maintenance of infrastructure,

whilst recognising the interdependence of all three and the importance of their integration.

In a democracy, governance and planning are clearly participatory processes that engage all those who have a stake in decisions that are made, usually through a system of representation, though direct democracy (referenda, 'town-hall meetings', community assemblies, etc.) has an important place in many decision-making processes, particularly those involving, and within, low-income urban communities, most of which are highly diverse, embracing social minority groups and majorities, women, men, young and old, all with different needs, ambitions and allegiances.

Managing the implementation of development plans through programmes and projects, particularly in low-income neighbourhoods, is increasingly being shown to benefit from partnership arrangements between the funders/financiers (generally government or international agencies), regulators (local government) and the beneficiaries (communities).

The administration of service charges for day-to-day utility delivery (water, sanitation, power, etc.) has also often been shown to be more efficient (affordable) when undertaken, at least in part, by the user communities, either in profit-sharing partnerships or through subcontracting arrangements with service providers. Solid waste management and the maintenance of local infrastructure (street drains, local public open space, access ways, etc.) and other community assets are generally more efficient and effective when in local control.

Invariably the introduction of any real participation or partnership in the planning and management of cities and the maintenance of its infrastructure and services entails a degree of decentralisation of responsibility and authority.

What Is Decentralisation?

'*Decentralisation*', a frequently loosely used term, embraces a range of different concepts and meanings. At one end of the scale are approaches such as de-concentration and decongestion in which responsibility for the implementation of centrally made decisions are dispersed to decentralised authorities or provincial outposts of a national ministry or agency.

'*Privatisation*', an extension of this form of decentralisation, is the process whereby managerial and administrative responsibilities are contracted out to private sector enterprises. The privatisation of traditionally public functions swept much of the world in the late 1980s and early 1990s under the rubric of structural adjustment programmers (SAPs) espoused by the World Bank and several bilateral donor agencies in the belief that the profit motive that drives private enterprise ensures efficient performance. However, negotiating contracts and maintaining quality control over privatised service delivery is complex and in many situations has produced some highly questionable results, particularly in terms of social equity and its impact on poverty.

'*Deregulation*', the loosening of central controls on standards and procedures, is closely allied to processes of decentralisation and privatisation. In the field of housing and urban development and management, deregulation also has been a mixed blessing. On one hand the deregulation of stringent rules and procedures has allowed for innovation and new initiatives in both technical and managerial aspects of housing and urban development, allowing new actors with new ideas into the process. On the other hand, the withdrawal of controls leading to the reduction of standards has often led to exploitation and excessive profiteering by the private sector.

3.2 Devolution

Devolution of authority differs significantly from the aspects of decentralisation outlined above. True devolution is not just the delegation of managerial or administrative responsibility; it is the handing down of decision-making powers from a higher authority (i.e. national or regional government) to 'lower' levels of decision-making (i.e. local government, neighbourhood and community organisations and beyond). Devolution underpins the processes of good governance in terms of its democratic (moral) imperative, its effectiveness and its efficiency. Effective, participatory decision-making depends upon people, communities and institutions being able to participate in the planning and management of the projects and programmes that directly affect them and their livelihoods. If decisions are made at too high a level or at too low a level their results are unlikely to be either effective – the wrong decisions will be made – or efficient –resources will be wasted. The principle of subsidiarity is central to the effective devolution of authority in the planning, management and administration of housing and urban development.

'*Subsidiarity*' is the recognition of the lowest effective level of decision-making. Emphasis here is on the word 'effective'. If authority is devolved to too low a level – one that does not represent the whole of the affected community – the results of decisions are unlikely to be either effective of efficient. Similarly, if decisions are made at too high a level, as is most common, it is unlikely that the values and priorities of those most affected will be well understood and their results will probably be both ineffective and inefficient. For instance, decisions about a dwelling can only effectively and efficiently be made at the level of the household;[6] those concerning a neighbourhood, such as the use and location of public open space, should be made at the level of the community that uses it; decisions to do with the distribution networks of water or power in a city can only be determined at the level of the municipality; and those concerning the impounding and bulk supply of water or power are decisions that must be taken at the regional or national level.

A move to decentralisation or devolution from central to local government swept many countries in the late 1980s and early 1990s.[7] However, rarely was the principle of subsidiarity fully recognised; hardly ever did the devolution process reach lower than municipal council level – down to the ward, neighbourhood or community, where many of the most fundamental decisions concerning poor people's lives and livelihoods should be made. There are notable exceptions, however. For instance: in 2003 in Thailand the Community Organisation Development Institute (CODI) under the National Housing Authority set up the Baan Mankong Programme for the management of a housing fund that was administered through a federated structure engaging some 300,000 households in 2,000 communities in 200 towns and cities. Local government in Ghana operates through 110 district and municipal assemblies, each embracing some 10–12 zonal or area councils, each made up of 12–14 locally elected unit committees, each representing a population of a little over 1,000 people or 200 households. In 2000 the government of South Africa charged every municipality with responsibility for preparing a five-year strategic development plan (to be reviewed annually) that responded to the needs of every section of society. This entailed a process not only of empowering municipalities but also ward committees, civil society organisations and community groups.

How to Devolve

There are two aspects to the process of devolving decision-making and managerial authority that are frequently confused: empowering and enabling.

Empowering is the act of devolving authority and granting legal instruments to organisations and agents to take responsibility for aspects of development and management – giving them the power to decide and act. Empowering is about increasing the efficiency, enhancing the effectiveness and ensuring the sustainability of development by passing responsibility to those people, communities and enterprises to whom efficiency, effectiveness and sustainability really matter.

However, frequently the actors at the level of decision-making to which authority should be devolved – the level that engages the greatest number of users or beneficiaries – are not adequately equipped to take on the responsibility that is devolved to them. They do not have adequate professional or technical understanding, or access to appropriate advisors – managerial and administrative capacity is lacking; they do not have adequate or appropriate organisational structures; etc. Thus they are not able to effectively exercise the power that has been devolved to them unless, together with their empowering, they have access to appropriate and responsive enabling supports.[8]

Enabling is ensuring that those who are empowered have the information, technology, skills and support to exercise their new authority (power) responsibly. It is about roles: understanding who should do what and in partnership with whom. Therefore it is also about relationships and interfacing between the different fields and the different levels of responsibility.

Thus the process of devolving authority must start by identifying the appropriate levels,[9] organisations and institutions to which any aspect of the planning, production and management of urban housing should be devolved, based on the principle of subsidiarity. Against each of these, the type of enabling support required can be charted, together with how and by whom this support will be provided. This may be summarised as in a Table 3.1, below.

In short, the fundamental objective of providing enabling supports is to build the capacity of communities, agencies and institutions in the appropriate levels and fields of housing and urban governance and management (see Chapter 9).

Table 3.1 Subsidiarity responsibilities

Component of housing production/management (activity, task)	Responsibility – Who (level, organisation, institution)			Support to be provided	
	Decides	Implements	Pays	What	By whom
Component 1					
Component 2					
Component 3, etc.					

3.3 Enabling Supports – Sites and Services and Informal Settlement ('Slum') Upgrading

The interpretation of devolution and the enabling paradigm for urban low-income group housing into policy and strategies for its implementation in the early 1970s embraced two types of activity by governments or municipal housing authorities, broadly under the rubric of 'non-conventional' approaches to housing production, maintenance and management: first, the provision of developed land and technical, managerial and social supports for the development of new housing; and, second, the upgrading of physical infrastructure and the provision of social and managerial supports in areas of substandard environmental conditions and housing in order to bring them to a socially acceptable standard.

By engaging the participation of the beneficiaries, both strategies devolved many aspects of decision-making and programme and project implementation to community leaders and householders, while retaining central control of city-level aspects such as project location and levels of infrastructure and service provision (Payne 1984).

Sites and Services (S&S)

Conceptually, the most simplistic application of the principle of subsidiarity applied to the procurement of affordable housing identified the basic division of responsibility as between those components that were most efficiently an effectively undertaken by government agencies and those that were best undertaken by the beneficiary households and communities.

Thus, at the project level, government housing agencies: acquired land; developed it with trunk, off-plot, infrastructure (water, sanitation, drainage, electricity, access ways and public open recreation space); subdivided it into residential plots with land reserved for public service and amenity buildings (education, health, cultural amenities, etc.); and allocated residential plots, with secure tenure, to the project-selected beneficiary households on affordable financial terms, who then would construct the superstructure of their dwellings, within the framework of any statutory or project-based conditions that may have been officially imposed. In many cases these stipulated the quality of permanent building materials that had to be used and in some cases, such as the Dandora project in Nairobi, Kenya, the floor plans that had to be followed (see Case Study 3, p. 41).

There were many interpretations of S&S, ranging from sites consisting of no more than four pegs in the ground, demarcating the corners of each plot and access to public water taps and pit-latrine sanitation, in some instances shared by as many as 30 households (150 people). In

Juba, South Sudan, sites were allotted on peri-urban land with unsurfaced access roads/paths and the promise that full infrastructure would be installed once the majority of plots were occupied and house construction had commenced. At the other extreme substantial government-constructed 'starter-homes', each consisting of a wet-service core (kitchen and bathroom) were provided with on-plot water-born sanitation and one or two living/sleeping rooms that beneficiary households could extend, as in the World Bank funded Jordan Urban Development Project in Amman in 1983–1987.

Case Study 3

Dandora, Nairobi, Kenya

The project, started in 1977, was the first major World Bank S&S venture in East Africa and its first ever to give major emphasis to community development as an integral part of the project's design and management. It grew out of a far-sighted Nairobi Metropolitan Growth Strategy formulated within Nairobi City Council (NCC). The site was on the eastern fringes of the city with easy access to the main industrial area. The project's first phase made 6,000 serviced plots available, each with a wet-services core, for three different income groups, the majority comprising of just a toilet, tap and shower. Loan finance for the construction of two additional rooms using unpaid self-help labour was provided. Community facilities included six primary schools, two health centres, markets, two community centres and a sports hall. Trunk infrastructure included paved roads with street lighting, water and a waterborne sewerage system. The project included 330 plots sold at market prices, the profit being used subsidise the cheapest plots to be allocated to the lowest income beneficiaries (Chana 1984).

The agreement with the World Bank stipulated that a special Project Department would be set up within NCC to manage the project. This was comprised of four divisions: Administrative; Legal, Technical and Community Development, with the last of these responsible for all aspects of public participation, working with, and providing training for, allottees before, during and after the occupation of their plots. The Community Development Division also coordinated independent local NGOs working with the project.

(continued)

(continued)

Strict conditions were imposed on the development of housing, including time limits for the construction of the extension of the wet-service cores with living and sleeping rooms, which had to be built of high quality, permanent materials (concrete floors with suitable damp proofing, rendered concrete block or dressed stone external walls, galvanised corrugated iron sheet roofs). Standard house plans were issued as guides to acceptable room sizes and layouts, including the positions of doors and windows. The smaller houses, intended for the lower-income group beneficiaries, had a minimum of two rooms. The guide plans for the middle-income and upper-income groups, on larger plots allowed for bigger houses. Beneficiaries of all income groups were encouraged to construct rooms for letting to tenants, with the intention of both providing rental accommodation for single people and small families, and to provide supplementary incomes to assist households to cover the cost of construction as well as to supplement their daily subsistence costs. As the project developed, it became apparent that the intended social benefits of mixing income groups, whilst recognising their different house-size needs, were not being realised. The upper-income households, many of whom had higher levels of education, tended to dominate the lower-income households in the emerging leadership roles and community decision-making and management. They also benefited to a greater extent in their ability to provide rental accommodation and therefore, in attracting tenants. As a result, social divisions developed, leading to animosity between income groups, and these divisions were beyond the control of the NCC Community Development Division advisory field staff (Lee-Smith & Memon 1988).

Nevertheless, despite a period of environmental deterioration in the 1990s, by 2017, 40 years after the project was started, Dandora had become a thriving, socially cohesive suburb of Nairobi with a strong local governance capacity and active community youth movement –the Dandora Transformation League.

Case Study 4

Kuda-ki-Bustee, Hyderabad, Pakistan

In 1986 the Hyderabad Development Authority (HDA) set out to simplify the provision of affordable housing to the lowest income groups by replicating, as closely as possible, the informal housing process practiced by low-income households in the city. The HDA allocated land in a 'conventional' S&S project (Gulshan-e-Shahbaz Scheme) on the urban fringes and subdivided it into some 3,000 plots, grouped in 'blocks' (neighbourhoods) that it advertised to very low-income home-less households in the city. Eligible applicants were then housed in reception areas for two weeks in very basic conditions, to 'test their resilience and seriousness'. Those who 'passed the test' of staying in the reception areas were then each allocated an $80m^2$ plot with no infra-structure (water was delivered daily by tanker) for a payment of US$30. Beneficiaries had to live on their plots in basic temporary shelters, gener-ally made of reeds, thatch and waste materials, while they progressively constructed a more permanent dwelling on the plot. No construction standards were imposed. To avoid speculation, plots were repossessed by HDA if they were not occupied. Beneficiaries were encouraged to pay instalments into a fund to cover the cost of infrastructure, which was provided once house construction had commenced on a majority of the plots in a 'block' and payments into the fund had been made. Domestic infrastructure networks (water and sewerage) were installed in each block by voluntary community participation, with organisa-tional and managerial supports and training provided by local NGOs.

After eight years around 2,800 plots had been allotted with a popu-lation of c. 18,000 people; five doctors provided health services with a permanent health care unit of the Family Planning Association of Pakistan; private buses to central Hyderabad and industrial locations plied every 30 minutes; there were 110 shops; more than 247 carpet looms provided jobs to at least 600 persons; residents had collected and spent some US$1.5 million on water supply, sewerage and elec-trification; every house had electricity and an indoor connection to a pipe-born water supply; more than 2,000 houses had been built with permanent materials (nearly all families had started with reed huts); and c. 70 collateral-free loans for enterprise development to a total value of c. US$27,000 had been disbursed, benefiting c.150 families.

The most significant characteristics of this approach were: the minimal capital outlay and management overheads by HDA and 'mimicking' the informal settlement process that made the pro-gramme affordable and sustainable. However a significant amount of capital, invested in the installation of infrastructure at the start of the 'conventional' S&S projects of the Gulshan-e-Shahbaz Scheme, was lost through deterioration due to lack of use before house connections were made. The Kuda-ki-Bustee scheme was most successful in the

(continued)

(continued)

blocks where NGOs had helped to organise community leadership and management right from the start.

The most important instruments used by HDA in the Kuda-ki-Bustee scheme were: its incremental nature; the continuous availability of plots, aided by the issuing of dwelling permits only when permanent construction had started, so that vacant houses/plots could be reallocated; and a simple, one-window bureaucratic procedure, performed on the spot (UNCHS 1991).

'Slum' Upgrading

In basic neighbourhood upgrading programmes, government housing agencies redeveloped local, off-plot infrastructure and service provision to socially acceptable standards. In some upgrading programmes technical, financial and legal (security of tenure) supports were also provided to individual householders for the individual upgrading of their dwellings. An innovative and interesting approach to upgrading was the Bombay Buildings Repairs and Renewal Board,[10] referred to in Section 2.2. The Board was established in 1970 to repair and to improve sanitation and structural safety in old central-city multi-storey tenements ('chawls') that provided single-room accommodation for thousands of low-income families and enterprises in the city centre.

'Chawls' were four and five storey buildings, constructed at the turn of the nineteenth/twentieth centuries of a heavy timber structural frame with brick infill (see Figure 2.5, p.26). Typically, they were c. 6 m wide and c. 30 m deep, with four or five rooms ranged on either side of a central corridor on each floor, each room housing a family or small industry. A sanitary area and access staircase, serving all occupants, was located at the back end of the corridor on each floor. By the 1950s, the timber structure of many chawl buildings was tending to rot, particularly around the sanitary area, where water had been allowed to stand, and on the south and west facades of the buildings, which faced the annual monsoon winds and rain. In the eight years from 1960–1968 some 1,130 such buildings had collapsed, or partially collapsed, killing almost 200 people and seriously injuring nearly 700. In 1956, there were 12,000 such buildings in the city with an expected safe lifespan of less than 15 years. This interesting example was unique to the particular circumstances of Bombay (Mumbai). The majority of slum upgrading programmers targeted lower density squatter shack settlements.

As with S&S projects, the range of standards and quality of infrastructure varied widely. Initially, upgrading programmes were designed to do little more than to ensure adequate access to potable water and safe sanitation and solid waste disposal and, in some projects, to include

Figure 3.1 Bombay (Mumbai), India, (1974). Chawl building undergoing
renovation by the Bombay Buildings Repairs and Renewal Board.
(Photo: Patrick Wakely)

all-weather access ways (footpaths and roads) and street lighting, as in the
Oshakati Human Settlements Improvement Programme (OHSIP) project in
Oshakati, Namibia, described in Section 4.3. In other settlement upgrading
programmes, government support extended to financial and technical assistance to individual households for the improvement of their dwellings, as
in the Urban Sub-programme of the Sri Lanka Million Houses Programme,
described in Section 4.1. As experience increased, settlement upgrading
programmes also embraced the provision of support to social development
and community governance and management skills, as well as employment
opportunities (Imparato & Ruster 2003).

So by the end of the twentieth century, in many cities S&S and neighbourhood upgrading had taken on a wider role in urban development strategies
than just the provision of access to well-serviced affordable shelter
and convivial neighbourhoods. At least in theory, they became treated

Figure 3.2 Wanatamulla (Seevalupura), Colombo, Sri Lanka, (1983), Infrastructure upgrading by 'Community Contract'. (Photo: Patrick Wakely)

Figure 3.3 Wanatamulla (Seevalupura), Colombo, Sri Lanka, (1985). Access path after upgrading by a 'community contract' and maintained regularly by the community organisation (CDC). (Photo: Patrick Wakely)

as significant components of wider programmes of urban social development and poverty alleviation and reduction. Though few national poverty reduction strategies made clear distinctions between urban poverty and rural or 'general' poverty, the participatory processes of initiating and implementing urban S&S and slum upgrading programmes and projects took on greater importance than just the resulting housing products (Ramirez 2002). They were seen as fundamental to urban poverty reduction and the alleviation of its impact, good urban governance and administration, fostering transparency and accountability in urban political decision-making and administrative practices (Frediani 2007). Nevertheless by the late 1990s, S&S projects had been sweepingly declared 'unsuccessful' and were virtually abandoned by governments and international aid agencies, alike.

Case Study 5

Parcelles Assainies, Dakar, Senegal

The first urban World Bank S&S project in Senegal called Parcelles Assainies, began in Dakar in 1972. The site was a vacant area dominated by sand dunes north of Dakar. The Office d'Habitat de Loyers Moderes (OHLM) planned to use World Bank 50-year US$8 million interest-free loans to develop 14,000 house plots of 150 square metres on 400 hectares of land, with an average occupancy rate of ten people per household. The project included minimal infrastructure with unpaved roads and just sufficient public spaces, schools, health clinics and community centres to serve 140,000 people. Beneficiaries bought their plots and their infrastructure through savings and/or a 15-year loan at 7 per cent interest, and then built their homes, using their own (contracted) technical resources.

The project was intended to house the very poorest families but initially it only reached down to the 47th income percentile. After some procedural adjustments, the majority of plot purchasers fell between the 20th and 65th income percentiles. The project start was delayed by disagreements between the government of Senegal and the World Bank to the extent that, by 1978 only 20 households had actually moved in. Major cuts to the project budget had been made in 1976, reducing the size of the site to 300 hectares and cutting back on education, health and community facilities. The political need for plots to be occupied, coupled with corruption (for example, 1,000 occupant households never went through the official selection process), meant that better-off people dominated.

(continued)

(continued)

In 1974 the President of Senegal, Leopold Senghor, visited the project and declared that all dwellings should have an individual water supply and water-born sanitation connections. This significantly increased costs to beyond the affordability of the target low-income group and signalled official approval for the allocation of plots to middle- and upper-income beneficiaries. By 1976 the first tranche of 3,500 households had been allocated plots *(parcelles)* and the roads, water supply and sewerage system were slowly being built. The project was wound up in 1981–1982, five years later than planned.

The project designers 'did not explicitly examine the projected level of density of the project from the perspective of the medium- or long-term time frame; and . . . they did not consider the planned settlement in terms of the wider patterns of land use existing in the city at the time. Rather, decisions on density were project-specific and disconnected from the urban context as a whole. [Nevertheless] in 1982, the World Bank and the Senegalese Government agreed that the project had been 'completed', as the momentum of occupancy and construction had increased considerably' (Cohen 2007).

3.4 Limits of the 'Self-help' and the Participation Paradigm

Of course, not all S&S projects ultimately led to success. Many mistakes were made, common amongst which was a lack of understanding of the importance of location. In their drive to reduce capital costs, many housing authorities acquired cheap undeveloped land on the city fringes at long distances from trunk infrastructure networks, transport routes and other services. Thus the level of infrastructure provision, notably water supply, was invariably costly and frequently inadequate. In addition, beneficiary households were far removed from their city-based social networks and from potential centres of urban employment and markets. So, the initial take-up of many such projects was low and they remained underdeveloped for this reason.

Another frequent mistake was the imposition of unaffordably high planning and construction standards. Fearful of accusations of officially condoning or supporting the development of 'new slums', many housing authorities imposed conditions on builder-households that dictated space standards, the use of stipulated, high-quality building materials and time limits for the completion of construction, many of which many low-income householders could not afford or meet, further jeopardising the take-up of S&S projects.

In addition, financial conditions for the recovery of the capital cost of land and infrastructure were often based on erroneous assumptions of affordability and poor urban households' ability/willingness to pay for them. For instance, several World Bank-financed S&S projects used social survey data from existing low-income (informal) settlements to establish households' ability to pay for housing (e.g. 25 per cent of annual household income), which was used to compute the repayment rate for the recovery of the capital costs of land and infrastructure, ignoring the additional cost that would be incurred by constructing habitable dwellings. In many cases this led to severe financial hardship and/or the lack of take-up and abandonment of the housing.

Such project-level problems compounded a more universal misunderstanding that in part led to the discrediting and eventual abandonment of participatory 'non-conventional' approaches to support for incremental 'self-help' housing production in many cities. This was the process by which they were evaluated – too soon and using the wrong criteria. Many projects were evaluated only two or three years after the initial construction stages, ignoring the length of time (up to 15–20 years) that it took most households and communities to fully develop their dwellings and neighbourhoods. Such evaluations tended to use the criteria/indicators that were generally employed to assess 'conventional' building projects, such

Figure 3.4 Las Colinas, Bogotá, Colombia (1972). New high-quality brick house being built around the 'first' house of impermanent construction. (Photo: Patrick Wakely)

as quality of construction and building materials. Almost invariably, in the first months and even years after occupation, S&S projects had the appearance and character of illegal informal settlements under construction – their occupants living and working in temporary shelters, often put together with second-hand and impermanent building materials and components, while building their permanent structures around them.

Revisiting S&S projects 20–30 years after their occupation, however, generally provides a very different picture – frequently one of thriving urban communities and neighbourhoods, not of half-built, self-help settlements that they would have been a few years after the start of their initial construction stage (see Case Studies 6–8).

Case Study 6

Guacamayas, Bogotá, Colombia

A S&S project started in 1976 by the Caja de Vivienda Popular (municipal housing authority) on the city fringes but with good access to the city centre and industrial areas.

1976 Core service units with one room on each plot were provided by the project. Many households moved onto the site with second-hand building materials and components to start extending their dwellings immediately. (Photo: Patrick Wakely)

1977 Within one year several families had 'customised' and extended their houses to include a second floor. (Photo: Patrick Wakely)

2010 Barrio Guacamayas had become fully urbanised, with traffic confined to perimeter roads and pedestrian precincts in the interiors of the blocks. Houses continued to be extended and improved. Guacamayas had its own community website: http://www.barrioguacamayas.com. (Photo: Maria Victoria Echeverri)

Case Study 7

Navagampura, Colombo, Sri Lanka

A S&S project initiated by the National Housing Development
Authority (NHDA) as part of the Million Houses Programme (MHP),
Urban Housing Sub-programme in 1985 on an inner-city site (see
Section 4.1).

1985 The project was laid out as terraced housing with shared 'party-walls'
between each dwelling – an innovation in Sri Lanka, where detached
houses on individual plots were the norm. (Photo: Patrick Wakely)

1986 The uniform roof level was spontaneously maintained by all builder-
households in the initial construction Stages. (Photo: Patrick Wakely)

2010 Navagampura had become a regular part of the urban fabric of Colombo and was still being developed by its residents. (Photo: Kumudu Jayaratne)

Case Study 8a

Ciudad Bachué, (Low-rise Housing) Bogotá, Colombia

Begun in 1977 by the national government housing agency, Instituto de Crédito Territorial (ICT), the incremental housing project had two

1979 Pre-fabricated concrete core houses. Households were already assembling traditional building materials for extensions, replacing doors and installing security grilles on windows. (Photo: Patrick Wakely)

(continued)

(continued)

components: low-rise terraced housing of concrete post and beam construction with pre-cast concrete wall panels and floor slabs, which householders could extend by building a second floor; and high-rise apartment/maisonette blocks (see Case Study 8b).

1985 Second-floor extensions were being added. Many of the pre-fabricated concrete panels were replaced with conventional block and brick construction. (Photo: Patrick Wakely)

1985 Second-floor extensions were being added. (Photo: Patrick Wakely)

2010 Roof terraces and third-floor extensions had been added. The house in the centre, being used as an informal nursery school, has not been extended and remains as the original precast concrete panel-constructed unit. (Photo: Patrick Wakely)

Case Study 8b

Ciudad Bachué, (High-rise apartments) Bogotá, Colombia

Three-storey apartment blocks with two-storey maisonettes (entered at ground level), which could be extended by building on plots at the

1978 Precast concrete columns and beams assembled. (Photo: Patrick Wakely)

(continued)

(continued)

rear of the block, and single storey apartments above (entered from open, third-floor access gallery), which could be extended by building on the roof.

1979 Maisonettes and apartments ready for occupation and extension. (Photo: Patrick Wakely)

1981 Extension of the apartments on the roof and maisonettes extended on plots at the rear of the block. (Photo: Patrick Wakely)

1987 Two-story extension on the roof and extensive 'personalisation'
(n.b: porch over the front-door and enclosed utility 'courtyard' on roof).
(Photo: Patrick Wakely)

2010 Residents collectively are responsible for the management and maintenance
of the common area between the fronts of the blocks, which several have
fenced-off creating gated semi-private enclaves. (Photo: Patrick Wakely)

In short, government-supported housing programmes and projects were stub-bornly regarded solely as construction activities and assessed by the quality (and capital cost) of the end product, alone. The impact of the process by which the housing product was procured was rarely considered amongst the objec-tives of such programmes and projects. In reaction to this, in 1972 John Turner coined the conceptual phrase 'housing as a verb – what housing does for peo-ple, rather than merely what it is' (Turner 1972) to emphasise the importance of user participation in the processes of the production, maintenance and management of housing to almost all aspects of urban social and economic development, as well as the quality and efficacy of the housing stock produced.

In addition and related to the perceived problems with the products of 'non-conventional' housing programmes and projects, they were generally judged as 'messy' and difficult to administer. For example, a World Bank review of its lending for urban projects in the mid-1970s recorded that shel-ter projects (largely S&S and some informal settlement upgrading) tended to take almost twice as long to disburse funds as other urban projects, such as transport, telecommunications and water supply. It made a strong point of the political and managerial difficulties of assembling land and securing the recovery of the costs of non-conventional 'self-help' housing programmes and projects (Cohen 1983).

In the early 1990s, the World Bank, and many other multilateral and bilateral aid agencies began to withdraw much of their support for 'non-conventional' housing strategies, particularly S&S projects, shifting support to the 'structural adjustment' of the management of national and metropoli-tan housing and urban policies as a whole, with some emphasis on easing private sector investment in housing and real estate development (World Bank 1993). Ultimately this led to renewed investment in 'conventional' contractor-built public housing and providing incentives to private sector developers, encouraging them to invest in new low-cost housing, accessible to the urban lower income groups at affordable prices. Government grants or guarantees were given to commercial banks and finance institutions to encourage them to provide mortgages to low-income borrowers at what were perceived to be higher levels of risk than was customary (see: Chapter 5).

Participatory approaches to the upgrading of existing sub-standard housing and neighbourhoods ('slums') did continue to be promoted and supported by international aid agencies and national governments in many countries, often as components of wider poverty alleviation and reduction programmes, but these did little to expand the urban housing stock or meet the growing demand for new affordable housing in urban areas, though, in many countries, it did reawaken the understanding of the social processes and values of urban housing production, maintenance and management and of its role as a vehicle for the development of community organisation and participatory local governance and administration, thus shifting the emphasis of public sector support to low-income housing into the field of social development, whilst still embracing the importance of technical innovation and physical place-making (Imparato & Ruster 2003).

An important conceptual underpinning of the 'non-conventional' housing paradigm was the freehold ownership of land and housing by owner-occupiers. Yet, as Alan Gilbert points out: 'One in three urban dwellers across the globe (one billion people) are tenants and in major cities [rental housing] often accommodates a majority of all households' (Gilbert 2008). For instance, in the 1980s 80 per cent of the households in Abidjan, Côte d'Ivoire, were tenants, the majority of them in informal settlements; in Port Harcourt, Nigeria 88 per cent were in rented accommodation. In India, 76 per cent of the population in Kolkata were renters and 68 per cent in Chennai (UN-Habitat 2005). Whilst the importance of outright freehold ownership of property as a stimulant to investment in its maintenance and development was recognised, a large proportion of the lowest urban income groups in any society or culture are unable or unwilling to take on the responsibility and imputed costs of the ownership of urban property, but are willing and able to meet the recurrent costs of renting accommodation.

Though much of the earlier 'conventional' public housing built by governments was let on a rental basis to its beneficiary occupants, in many countries, housing authorities, unable to meet the landlord costs and administrative burden of managing and maintaining rental housing for low-income tenants, sold their stock by outright purchase or entered into hire-purchase arrangements with beneficiary households (Gilbert 2008) and/or launched into 'non-conventional' approaches to the production of housing for urban low-income groups with freehold title, leaving the production, maintenance and management of rental accommodation to the private sector. However, renting to the lowest urban income groups is rarely financially attractive to formal sector developers and landlords and has often led to widespread exploitation, thereby giving 'landlordism' and the whole low-income rental housing business a bad name. It is thus left to the informal sector, where the renting of accommodation not only fulfils a market demand for affordable housing but also typically provides an important source of income to a new category of 'subsistence landlords', who are often in the same low-income group, or poorer, than their tenants (Kumar 1996).

Notes

1 In a paper delivered to a conference on Development Policies and Planning in Relation to Urbanisation at the University of Pittsburgh, USA and published by the United Nations (Turner, 1968); expanded upon later in John Turner's book *Housing by People* (1976).

2 Notably, the World Bank, United Nations Development Programme (UNDP), the Regional Development Banks (ADB, IDB, AfDB, CDB) and European and North American bilateral aid agencies and later, in 1978, the UN Centre for Human Settlements (UNCHS), upgraded to UN Human Settlements Programme (UN-Habitat) in 1985.

3 Arnstein's ladder: 1. Manipulation; 2. Therapy; 3. Informing; 4. Consultation; 5. Placation; 6) Partnership; 7. Delegated power; 8. Citizen control (Arnstein 1969).

4 Otto Koenigsberger, Charles Abrams, John F.C. Turner and others had been advocating participation in urban housing for more than a decade before 1976 (see, for example: Abrams 1964; Mangin 1967; Turner & Fichter 1972).

5 It may be argued that 'co-production' is a separate stage that comes between Mark 2 Participation and partnerships. As discussed by Diana Mitlin (2008) co-production arrangements have almost invariably been initiated by community initiatives or action that is condoned and then supported by the state on an *ad hoc* basis, rather than being initiated by government as part of public policy.

6 Strong arguments exist for the extension of the subsidiarity principle below that of the 'household' to take into account the different age and gender needs of women an men, girls and boys that make up a household group (Moser & Peake 1987).

7 For example in 1992 the 74th amendment to the Indian constitution devolved many central government and state powers to municipalities; in Colombia Ley 9[a] of 1989 gave municipalities the power to elect mayors and councils and take on responsibilities that had hitherto been the responsibility of national government. In Ghana in 1988 local government reform (PNDC Law 207) led to the establishment district and municipal assemblies, zonal councils and unit committees, each at a different level in the hierarchy of devolved authority with commensurate responsibilities.

8 The devolution of authority under the 74th amendment of the Indian constitution was seriously questioned and calls were made for the recentralisation of powers in several states because of the inability of local authorities to exercise their functions adequately. They had been empowered, but not enabled.

9 In the interests of brevity, the discussion on subsidiarity and devolution uses the term 'level' as a shorthand for the complex range of different interest and needs groups in a city, such as gender, age, ethnic and social identity, faith, etc., including organisational hierarchies, such as metropolitan, municipal, ward, neighbourhood, housing cluster, etc.

10 The Board, financed by Bombay municipality, compulsorily undertook/contracted the repairs/rebuilding on all chawl buildings, certified unsafe, recovering most of the cost from a levy (of 10 per cent of rateable value) on the landlords of all rented residential buildings in the city (c. 36,000), plus a small contribution from the occupants (tenants) of the improved chawl buildings.

References

Abrams, C. 1964, *Housing in the Modern World: Man's Struggle for Shelter in an Urbanising World*, MIT Press, Cambridge MA, USA.

Arnstein, S.R. 1969, 'A ladder of citizen participation', *Journal of the American Institute of Planners*, Vol. 35, No. 4, Washington DC, USA.

Chana, T. 1984, 'Nairobi: Dandora and other projects', in Payne, G.K (ed.) *Low-Income Housing in the Developing World: The Role of Sites and Services and Settlement Upgrading*, Wiley, Chichester, UK.

Cohen, M., 1983, *Learning by Doing: World Bank Lending for Urban Development 1972–82*, The World Bank, Washington DC, USA

Cohen, M., 2007, 'Aid, density and urban form: Anticipating Dakar', *Built Environment*, Vol. 33, No. 2, Alexandrine Press, Oxford, UK.

Frediani, A. 2007, 'Amartya Sen, the World Bank and the redress of urban poverty: A Brazilian case study', *Journal of Human Development*, Vol. 8, No. 1, Routledge, Abingdon, UK.

Gilbert, A., 2008, 'Slums, tenants and home-ownership: On blindness to the obvious', *International Development Planning Review*, Vol. 30, No. 2, Liverpool, UK.

Imparato, I. & J. Ruster, 2003, *Slum Upgrading and Participation: Lessons from Latin America*, The World Bank, Washington DC, USA.

Kumar, S., 1996, 'Subsistence and petty-capitalist landlords: A theoretical framework for the analysis of landlordism in Third World low-income settlements', *International Journal of Urban and Regional Research*, Vol. 20, No. 2, Wiley, London, UK.

Lee-Smith, D. & Memon, P., 1988, 'Institution development for delivery of low-income housing: An evaluation of Dandora Community Development Project in Nairobi', *Third World Planning Review*, Vol. 10, No. 3, Liverpool, UK.

Mangin, W., 1967, 'Latin American squatter settlements: A problem and a solution', *Latin American Research Review*, Vol. 2.

Mitlin, D., 2008, 'With and beyond the state: Co-production as a route to political influence, power and transformation for grass-roots organizations', *Environment & Urbanization*, Vol. 20, No. 2, Sage, London, UK.

Moser, C. & L. Peake (eds) 1987, *Women, Human Settlements and Housing*, Tavistock, London, UK.

Payne, G.K., 1984, 'Introduction' in Payne, G.K (ed.) *Low-Income Housing in the Developing World: The Role of Sites and Services and Settlement Upgrading*, Wiley, Chichester, UK.

Ramirez, R., 2002, *Urban Poverty Reduction and Urban Security Consolidation: A New Paradigm at Work? A Review of Theory and Practice*. UN-Habitat/UNDP/World Bank Urban Management Programme (UMP) Working Paper Series No. 20, Nairobi, Kenya.

Riley, E. & P. Wakely, 2005, *Communities and Communication: Building Urban Partnerships*, ITDG Publishing, Rugby, UK.

Turner, J.F.C., 1968, 'Uncontrolled urban settlement: Problems and policies', International Social Development Review No. 1, *Urbanization: Development Policies and Planning*, United Nations, New York, USA.

Turner, J.F.C., 1976, *Housing by People: Towards Autonomy in Building Environments*, Marion Boyars, London, UK.

Turner, J.F.C. & R. Fichter, 1972, *Freedom to Build: Dweller Control of the Housing Process*, Macmillan, New York, USA.

62   *Enabling Support Strategies*

UNCHS, 1991, *The Incremental Development Scheme: A Case Study of Kuda-Ki-Bustee in Hyderabad, Pakistan*, UNCHS Training Materials Series No. HS/232/91E, UN-Habitat, Nairobi, Kenya.

UN-Habitat, 2005, *Financing Urban Shelter: Global Report on Human Settlements 2005*, Earthscan, London, UK.

World Bank, 1993, *Housing: Enabling Markets to Work*, World Bank Policy Paper, Washington DC, USA.

4 Three Case Studies of Enabling Support Strategies

This chapter reviews three very different examples of sustained programmes of government support to participatory enabling approaches to the procurement of affordable urban housing, services and infrastructure by the lowest income groups. The first two examine the implementation of national and metropolitan level policies; the third recounts in some project-level detail the setting up and implementation of an informal settlements upgrading project in a relatively small town:

1 The Urban Housing Sub-programme of the Sri Lanka Million Houses Programme (MHP) by the National Housing Development Authority (NHDA) (1983–1989) that embraced extensive production of new urban dwellings through community-based sites and services projects as well as the upgrading of existing informal neighbourhoods;
2 The Rio de Janeiro Favela Bairro programme of the Rio Municipal Housing Department (SMH), based on urban regeneration and the upgrading of physical and social infrastructure in informal neighbourhoods (*favelas*) and communities (1999–2004);
3 The Oshakati Human Settlements Improvement Programme (OHSIP) in Namibia by the Oshakati Town Council, supported by a Danish non-governmental development organisation (NGDO) with Danish International Development Agency (DANIDA) grant aid funding (1991–1995).

4.1 The Sri Lanka Million Houses Programme

Context

Prior to 1980, Sri Lanka's urban social housing policy entailed the administration of rent control legislation intended to ensure a supply of rental housing affordable to low-income urban households and the production of 'conventional' rented public housing, most of it in three- or four-storey apartment blocks, built by direct construction. In addition, in 1973, following a period of unusually high population growth in Greater Colombo,[1] largely due to migration from rural areas, the government[2] enacted the Ceiling on Housing Property Law, intended to address the problem of exploitative urban landlords, many of whom owned large numbers of small tenements that were under-serviced and dilapidated through lack of maintenance, largely as a result of the stringent constraints imposed by the rent control laws. The new law was also intended to introduce a measure of redistribution in the ownership of urban property to the lower income groups in the city by transferring the title of properties in excess of two per owner to the occupying tenants[3] (Weerapana 1986).

In 1978 the newly elected 'social-democratic' United National Party government launched the One Lakh (Hundred Thousand) Houses Programme, with the mandate to construct 100,000 dwellings, largely in rural areas throughout the country by sites and services (S&S) and organised (aided) self-help (ASH) projects. The programme was administered by the newly created NHDA under the then minister of Local Government, Housing and Construction, Ranasinghe Premadasa, who was later appointed prime minister of Sri Lanka. The houses were allocated to low-income families by members of parliament through an Electoral Housing Programme – a process with little transparency or accountability.

The One Lakh Houses Programme was unable to meet its numerical target of 100,000 dwellings by the end of the government's first five-year term in office, but such was the political capital built up around it, that rather than abandon public support for self-help approaches to housing production by the lowest income groups, the minister went a step further and launched the MHP, with the promise to have supported the construction or upgrading of one million dwellings by low-income households and communities themselves within five years. Meeting such a target required a substantial revision of the centrally controlled and direct-labour-led ASH mode of housing production employed by the One Lakh Houses Programme. It took the form of confining government intervention to the provision of small incremental loans and basic technical advice and training to low-income households for the construction and/or improvement of their dwellings and neighbourhood infrastructure.

Correspondingly, the management and technical capacities of the NHDA, which already operated through a decentralised structure of district offices in each of the 25 administrative districts in the country, had to be overhauled and 're-tooled'. This process was initiated through a hierarchy of 'inter-facing' training workshops, in which the new policy was described and its implementation strategies discussed by NHDA head office senior officers and political leaders and senior government administrative officers in each region of the country; then the regional political and administrative leaders introduced the programme strategies to the NHDA district managers (DMs) and district-level supervisory staff, in the presence of their superiors; the process was then repeated with the DMs instructing field-level technical operatives and so on down to the level of community organisations and supporting non-governmental organisations (NGOs). This cascade process[4] was highly effective in ensuring the transparency and accountability of each level in the hierarchy of authority, in engaging each level of actors in refining the MHP policy and integrating each stage of its implementation in each district and urban centre in the country (Lankatilleke 1986).

At its start the MHP only addressed housing in rural areas. Housing in Colombo and other major urban areas was the responsibility of the Slum and Shanty Division (SSD) of the Urban Development Authority (UDA), also part of the Ministry of Local Government, Housing and Construction. In 1985 the UDA SSD was transferred to the NHDA and the MHP Urban Sub-Programme was launched with a Housing Options and Loans Package (HOLP) and a set of Operational Guidelines that embraced both the upgrading of existing urban slums and shanties and the provision of S&S on hitherto undeveloped urban land. It also included security of tenure to the land on which a house was to be built or upgraded for the duration of the loan amortisation period, initially set at 15 years – in effect a type of hire-purchase arrangement.

Programme Operation

The basic unit of management of the programme was a Community Development Council (CDC), a community-based NGO in each slum or shanty settlement, that was expected to have a locally recognised/elected leadership and management structure (chairperson, secretary, treasurer, locally accepted decision-making processes and regularly minuted meetings open to all neighbourhood residents). CDCs had already been set up in many under-served settlements in Colombo and other major urban centres in Sri Lanka by the UDA SSD and a United Nations Children's Fund (UNICEF)-supported Urban Basic Services Programme in the 1970s, but by 1985 they had no active function, though many of them were still in place, ready to be co-opted by the MHP Urban Housing Sub-Programme. As part of the programme they were responsible for the administration of small 'soft' loans to individual householders for the construction and/or improvement of their dwellings[5] and for the upgrading of neighbourhood infrastructure and services by communities, with oversight and technical and managerial training provided by the local NHDA District Office.

Figure 4.1 Colombo, Sri Lanka (1987), city central area slum. (Photo: Patrick Wakely)

Through the intensive training programme, described above, and on-the-job learning, DMs were converted from being the managers of public sector construction enterprises to the managers of housing and infrastructure loan funds and supervisors of small loans distribution and recovery and the administration of field-level technical assistance and training advisors. Housing officers, previously responsible for construction site technical supervision, became community development organisers and technical advisors to builder-householders and/or their contracted artisans and labourers, and so on.

Figure 4.2 Colombo, Sri Lanka (1987), MHP Urban Sub-programme, central city slum house upgrading. (Photo: Patrick Wakely)

Programme Outcomes

By-and-large, the process worked well, particularly at the level of constructing or improving individual dwellings; slightly less so for the development of neighbourhood infrastructure and services, though there were many examples of highly successful 'community contracts', through which CDCs tendered for and won contracts for neighbourhood-level public infrastructure works, funded by the NHDA (see Figures 3.2 and 3.3, p. 46). There was widespread dissatisfaction with the 15-year lease on land by householders who found it difficult to make repayments on their housing loans in so short a time and whose ultimate ambition was to have full freehold ownership title to their property. So, under political pressure, the duration of the NHDA lease was extended from 15 years to 30 years, then to 50 years by the minister, against the advice of several of his technical staff; and in 2008 all previously awarded MHP leases were commuted to full freehold title in perpetuity, with no further payments.

An important lesson learnt from the Sri Lanka MHP was the importance of effective and well-managed community-based organisations (CBOs) (CDCs) and their ability to communicate with and work in partnership with government agencies, in this case the NHDA district offices and urban local authorities (Riley & Wakely 2005). Concomitant with this was the capacity of the NHDA to initiate and provide appropriate and adequate community development and management support/assistance and training to CBOs (Sirivardana 1986).

A fundamental principle that underpinned community participation in house building/improvement and neighbourhood infrastructure development/upgrading was the importance of regular household saving. Initially, this was managed by the CDCs that collected, banked and kept accounts for small sums, usually deposited by the senior women in each participating household. In Colombo in the early 1990s, several CDCs, with NGO support, came together to manage these deposits as a collective cooperative mutual savings-and-loans fund, called the Praja Sahayaka Service. Over time, this developed into a national cooperative Women's Bank, which had strict rules to protect its original principles as a financial service for organised groups of poor women. By 1995 the Sri Lanka Women's Bank had 20 branches and some 5,600 members, representing almost 600 savings groups in urban low-income group settlements throughout the country. By the turn of the century the Women's Bank had grown to more than 250 branches with capital holdings of Rs5 billion (US$35.3 million), serving some 80,000 individual women members.

Another important process was community action planning (CAP), an analytical brainstorming activity led by NGOs that engaged all residents in establishing priorities for the upgrading of slums and shanties and the roles of the principal actors in the development of new (S&S) housing (Hamdi & Goethert 1997).

4.2 Rio de Janeiro Favela Bairro Programme, Brazil

Context

The existence of informal squatter settlements (*favelas*) in Rio de Janeiro was first recorded in the 1890s. Epidemics of yellow fever and tuberculosis in the first years of the twentieth century drew attention to insanitary conditions in some city-centre areas of tenements that housed the poorest households in the city. This sparked a spate of slum clearances, forcing the evicted occupants to construct new informal *favelas* illegally on the city fringes and on central infill sites that remained undeveloped because of the dangerously steep hillside slopes on which they were located. This process was repeated in cycles that entailed the demolition of relatively newly established *favelas*, only to be replaced by even newer ones, so that by 1950 Rio's *favela* population amounted to 170,000 (7.5 per cent of the total city population of 2.3 million). Rio's *favelas* continued to grow in number, size and density throughout the twentieth century, most notably between 1930 and 1960, a period of extensive industrialisation and rural–urban migration in Brazil.[6] Throughout the first 80 years of the twentieth century, most notably during the period of military dictatorship (1964–1985), little attempt was made to improve environmental and social conditions in *favelas* in Rio. Policy, led by the federal government, continued to be one of *favela* clearance and forcible rehousing of occupants in public high-rise housing estates on the urban periphery. There were, however, occasional attempts at improving living conditions in well-established *favelas* through 'one-off' uncoordinated environmental upgrading projects and the extension of some welfare services to selected *favela* communities. As part of these *ad hoc* projects, residents associations were established with official municipal support to represent the affected communities in negotiations with government and utility authorities.

In the 1950s residents associations were set up in many *favelas* in Rio, in addition to those in which there were upgrading projects. The residents associations, the leaders of which were popularly elected, were formally institutionalised by the municipal government and recognised by official

Figure 4.3 Andaraí favela, Rio de Janeiro, Brazil (2003), upgraded as part of the 'Favela Bairro' programme. (Photo: Alberto Lopes)

utility agencies. In the 1970s coalitions of *favela* residents associations and other CBOs came together[7] to lobby for the termination of slum clearance activities throughout the city, replacing them with the *in-situ* upgrading of a greater number of *favelas*. The Rio de Janeiro state government responded to this demand by initiating a small number of pilot environmental upgrading projects. Many of these were successful and popular and by the beginning of the 1980s both state and municipal governments throughout Brazil were starting to adopt 'non-conventional' approaches to social housing provision. In 1983 the Rio de Janeiro State Water and Sanitation Company[8] reversed its longstanding policy of assuming no responsibility for servicing *favelas*, as they were considered 'illegal' settlements that should not be condoned or even recognised, and launched an ambitious sanitation upgrading programme to install water distribution networks and sewerage system connections in all *favelas* in the city. By 1986 the programme had benefited nearly 250,000 people in over 60 *favelas*.

Programme Operation

In the early 1980s land invasions began to increase dramatically both on the city fringes and in central areas of Rio, typically on land left undeveloped because of steep slopes and/or unstable surface conditions. The municipal government, then led by the Democratic Labour Party, in response to political pressure, initiated by the FANERJ coalition of *favela* residents associations (and a National Movement for Urban Reform), supported by the federal government, launched a programme called Rio Cidade (Rio City), together with a new city master plan, prepared by the Municipal Secretariat for Urban Affairs,[9] with the objective of transforming the entire infrastructure and image of the city, for which the city authorities earmarked over US$220 million to renew much of the city's infrastructure (water and sewerage networks, road improvements and street lighting). The master plan for the first time recognised the need to address low-income housing (and *favelas*) as an integral part of the overall city development strategy, rather than as a series of one-off local interventions.

The housing objectives of the plan embraced: the rationalisation of land use; the upgrading and legalisation of *favelas* and illegal subdivisions; the construction of subsidised 'conventional' public housing and the management of S&S projects. To meet these objectives, in 1993 the city government established a Municipal Housing Department (SMH),[10] which immediately launched the Favela Bairro programme, aiming to upgrade all of Rio's medium-sized *favelas* by 2004, to which were added two secondary programmes 'Bairreinho' and 'Grandes Favelas', respectively covering small and large *favelas*, thereby embracing all *favelas* in the city and on its peri-urban fringes.[11] The Favela Bairro programme was allocated a budget of US$120 million from the city's coffers plus another US$180 million loan from the Inter-American Development Bank (IDB). It explicitly set out to build upon the existing housing and infrastructure that had been built up informally, together with earlier government upgrading initiatives in the city's *favelas*. It was not intended to directly support the shelter needs of individual households but to address the collective needs of each *favela* as a whole, by:

- installing basic sanitation and circulation systems, enabling pedestrian and vehicular access to all dwellings and ensuring the effective and efficient provision of public services (environmental health, education and security);
- introducing 'urban symbols' of the formal city (paved roads, squares, tree-planting, recreation and cultural facilities);
- incorporating *favelas* into the planning and management process of the city as a whole, including its planning standards and development control legislation, development plans and programmes, maps and registers;

In addition to these physical aims, the Favela Bairro programme set out to:

- provide for and administer social and welfare services, including pre-school and child-care facilities, social, cultural and sports facilities, adult education and skill training opportunities and programmes; and
- provide recognised title to *favela* households and/or provide technical assistance to enable them to secure and demonstrate the legality of their tenure to the land and property that they occupied.

In short, the Favela Bairro programme aimed at improving the standard of living of *favela* dwellers by integrating them with the formal city, in the first instance by upgrading the physical infrastructure and latterly by administering urban utilities (water, sewerage and solid waste recycling/disposal, electricity and telecommunications) and social and welfare services (sport, culture and leisure, community centre facilities, adult education and skill training programmes, pre-school and child-care facilities, domestic and environmental health programmes). The overall objectives of the programme did not explicitly refer to it contributing to the reduction of poverty or the alleviation of its social impacts, but it did clearly recognise the programme's potential for 'improving the quality of peoples lives . . . and the significance of integrating the two parts of the city: the formal and the informal, by meeting the collective basic needs of both' (Magalhães 1997; and Ramirez 2002).

The implementation of the programme was firmly based on participation and the coordination (by SMH) of *favela* communities, the relevant public service authorities and NGOs, working with each *favela* community. Initially, the officially recognised residents associations, where they existed, provided community leadership and the point of contact between *favela* residents and the public sector officials. However, in several *favelas* the residents associations tended to lose their credibility with government departments and utility agencies due to their co-option by powerful drugs cartels and other criminal organisations, and/or cease to command the respect of their constituents and their local authority by becoming seen as being too close to government and 'the establishment' and thereby not able to adequately defend the interests of the communities that they ostensibly represented (Riley & Wakely 2005). Special-interest CBOs, ranging from religious groups to sports and leisure interest groups, that existed alongside the residents associations in most *favelas*, also played an active part in the Favela Bairro programme. A key part in the programme was played by architectural firms and practices that were responsible for overall project design and supervision in partnership with *favela* communities, usually represented by the residents associations. The sequence of work in each *favela* embraced four distinct stages, starting with diagnostic studies of existing conditions, based on professional/technical observation and the communities' stated priorities for improvement, leading to the preparation of outline plans and proposals for physical/environmental upgrading and the provision or enhancing of social facilities and economic opportunities, culminating with approval by the relevant utility authorities and SMH and the awarding of contracts for works, usually by competitive tenders by private sector engineering and construction companies, and the organisation of social and welfare services, coordinated by the municipal departments for culture, social development, education and employment.[12]

Although the architects retained responsibility for overall project supervision of works and coordination of the wide range of public, private and NGO actors, in many *favelas* SMH appointed its own project managers from amongst its technical staff, who acted as the architects' and contractors' 'clients' with overall budgetary and quality control responsibilities.

Programme Outcomes

By 2008, when SMH, with IDB support, undertook a formal evaluation of the impact of the Favela Bairro programme, upgrading projects had been completed in 168 *favelas*, mostly medium-sized *favelas*, but including some in small and large *favelas*. All infrastructure works had been satisfactorily undertaken, including the creation and planting of new public open spaces, squares, road grading and improvements and the construction

Figure 4.4 Santa Marta favela, Rio de Janeiro, Brazil (1998), public access way before upgrading. (Photo: Patrick Wakely)

Figure 4.5 Santa Marta favela, Rio de Janeiro, Brazil (2010), public access steps/anti-erosion storm-water drain upgrading by 'Favela Bairro' programme. (Photo: Patrick Wakely)

of safe pedestrian walkways and open hillside public access staircases. Social facilities, such as community centres, libraries, pre-school nurseries, schools, gymnasia and sports facilities had also been built in several *favelas*. This evaluation was somewhat mechanistic and concentrated on checking the 'hardware' components of each project against its initial terms-of-reference and goals. Nevertheless the outcome was impressively positive.

Other surveys by independent NGOs and academic institutions went into greater depth on the impacts of the social components of the programme, including satisfaction surveys of the physical upgrading of infrastructure, etc. The majority of these record general satisfaction with the improvements in living conditions that resulted from the implementation of the programme, particularly the security of tenure to property that it brought and, in several *favelas*, a substantial increase in the market value of property. Greater access to urban services and reliable supplies of water also featured amongst the most appreciated assets provided by the programme. Satisfaction with the participatory processes during the implementation of works (consultative community forums), leading to a strengthened sense of engagement in local governance and management and 'being listened to' were frequently expressed as indicators of the programme's success. In several *favelas*, people said that the implementation of the programme had strengthened the residents associations and improved their managerial abilities, which was considered to be 'a very good thing for everybody'. Few *favela*-dwellers were able to comment on the extent to which the programme had met its objective of 'integrating the *favela* with the formal city'. It was considered too early to judge this, even if people could recognise indicators by which to do so (Fiori & Brandao 2012). However, several architects and social development professionals who had been engaged with the programme recorded that there were clear indications of collective attitude-change and raised levels of morale (feelings of greater security) in many *favelas* as a result of the programme, but there was little indication of any reduction in the crime rate or drugs trade activities in the upgraded *favelas* (Fiori et al. 2001).

4.3 Oshakati Human Settlements Improvement Programme (OHSIP), Namibia

Context and Actors

Oshakati (population 37,000), capital of the relatively densely populated Owambo Region is located a few kilometres south of Namibia's border with Angola. Its economy depends upon local trading, much of it illegal cross-border smuggling, and its administrative functions as a regional capital. At Independence in 1990, the government of Namibia,[13] through the Ministry of Local Government and Housing (MLGH), gave emphasis to the development of the town because of its administrative and political importance and its strategic location on the northern border. This was also part of a strategy to help stem the migration of people from the densely populated northern regions of the country to the capital, Windhoek.

In 1991 the government signed an agreement with the Danish NGDO Ibis[14] for a three-year programme of support with DANIDA grant aid funds to improve the infrastructure, housing and the delivery of services in the informal settlements of Oshakati, in which some 70 percent of the town's population lived and worked. Addressing the high levels of unemployment and the creation of jobs were seen as central components of the proposal. It also recommended that the project should adopt a 'modified participatory approach' to community involvement. It was envisaged that this would help to speed up the slow process of participatory local development that the government's new National Development Policy espoused.

Shortly after signing the agreement for the OHSIP, the Namibian Local Authorities Act (1992) was passed and a new town clerk was appointed, followed by the election of the first Oshakati Town Council (OTC).

At the same time the government published the draft of a new National Housing Policy that gave emphasis to the involvement of private capital and enterprise across the whole sector, minimising public subsidies and adopting appropriate (affordable) planning and building standards in selected low-income group residential areas, in support of which, the MLGH launched a nationwide Build Together Programme with technical support from UNDP (United Nations Development Programme)/UNCHS (United Nations Human Settlements Programme). The Build Together Programme was closely modelled on the Sri Lanka MHP[15] described in Section 4.1.

Project Operation

In compliance with the draft National Housing Policy, the OTC started the OHSIP by constituting a Community Housing Development Group of elected town councillors and administrative department heads, to oversee the implementation of the programme, the cornerstone of which was the establishment or revival of community development committees[16] as the base level of non-governmental municipal management in each of the town's four large informal settlements.

It was assumed that the new OTC would welcome the establishment/ revival of the community development committees as they would be able to act as operational intermediaries between the OTC and its constituents

Figure 4.6 Oshakati Informal settlement in arid desertic environment.
(Photo: Gitte Jacobsen)

and ultimately would be able to take responsibility for the management and maintenance of local public infrastructure and community assets. However, the councillors had been elected by proportional representation of lists of candidates drawn up centrally by each political party, dominated by a large SWAPO[17] majority and did not represent, or identify with, any particular constituents, electoral ward or community in Oshakati. Furthermore, many councillors saw the community development committees as a threat to the authority of the OTC and, by extension, to their own political careers. Neither the principles nor the expediency of subsidiarity, upon which the project's participatory objectives were based, were fully understood or accepted during the early stages of the OHSIP.

The project received little operational support from OTC and the Community Housing Development Group never became much more than a disinterested, routine 'rubber-stamping' function that only met when procedurally required. Nevertheless, largely due to the efforts of the Ibis technical support team and a corps of community advisors delegated to the project by the Regional Directorate of Community Development, the early stages of the OHSIP shifted away from the engineering aspects of the physical upgrading of infrastructure and construction of dwellings, as set out in the original terms of reference, to community mobilisation and organisation for the local management of environmental development by a series of community development committee sub-committees in each informal settlement, each representing no more than 80 households. Each of these sub-committees was also constituted as a Community Credit Union to encourage households to start saving for the construction or improvement of their dwellings.

The first major task undertaken by the sub-committees was to conduct a local census in each of the large informal settlements embraced by the project and to map the commonly agreed boundaries of every householder's land. This was no easy task in the dense, irregular layouts of the settlements with no recognisable roads, paths or public spaces, and in which, over a long period of time, land had been allotted to new urban immigrant families by the traditional 'headmen' in exchange for a proverbial 'bottle of schnapps'. Nevertheless, it was an essential starting point in the process that would ultimately award householders secure title to their land, so that they could safely invest in house building and improvement, without fear of eviction. The precise delineation of boundaries between plots could only be determined by neighbouring householders themselves. This was seldom without dispute but always with resolution through arbitration by the community development committees. The agreed demarcations were recorded on diagrammatic maps and with marker pegs in the ground. This informal cadastre provided the basis for the next stage of local development: the alignment of roads, access ways and public spaces and the location of electricity, 'street light' posts and water mains and communal standpipes and the location of public amenities, notably a community centre in each settlement.[18]

The construction of community centres in each settlement and the clearing and aligning of local access roads, financed by DANIDA grant funds, provided the starting point for a sustained process of community contracting, managed by the community development committees, that generated paid employment as well as an institutional income for the community development committees. The principal enterprise was concrete block-making that, in one settlement, developed into a community development committee-run enterprise making concrete blocks employing over 100 women and men, which supplied not only the needs of the OHSIP but the town's formal private sector commercial building industry as well.

Among the most visible and important of the physical contributions of the OHSIP to environmental and family health was the design and construction of some 1,300 safe, thermally ventilated, odourless dry-disposal toilets that became named *Okakadis*,[19] to which any household was entitled on the payment of a small registration fee. Some 100 public water points (standpipes) with bathing and clothes-washing facilities operated

Figure 4.7 Oshakati OHSIP New houses built of concrete blocks, made by CDC
    Community Enterprise. (Photo: Gitte Jacobsen)

by a prepaid magnetic card system were installed, each serving 15–20
households that soon became neighbourhood meeting places, used particularly by women and children. Another highly appreciated service was
the connection of the settlements to the main power supply that enabled
the OHSIP to provide public street lighting on the newly demarcated
roads and public open spaces, including at the communal water points.
The public street lighting was popularly assumed to herald private house
connections.[20]

Project Outcomes

These physical achievements notwithstanding, the most significant and
popularly acclaimed impact of the OHSIP was its demonstration of the
effectiveness of community management and control of local development
processes. The community development committees that were 'inherited',
rather than those that were initiated by the project, were not all entirely
satisfactory: they had not been locally elected; some leaders had political
interests beyond the remit of the communities that they served; they had

few management skills and a slender notion of the principles of democratic governance. Yet, by mid-1994 the communities, backed by the local media, had expressed the need for democratically elected community development committees with approved constitutions and responsibilities. A drafting committee, chaired by the Oshakati town clerk was set up and, after an exhaustive process of popular and legal consultation, new committee constitutions were approved by the OTC and the national MLGH. Community development committees elections were held in 1995, a little over three years after the start of the project.

The OSHIP was declared a 'Global Best Practice' by the United Nations at the City Summit or UN Conference on Human Settlements (Habitat II) in Istanbul in 1996.

4.4 Lessons from the Case Studies

The first two case studies illustrate two very different approaches to the implementation of 'non-conventional' participatory urban housing policies, at a national level in the case of the Sri Lanka MHP and as a metropolitan policy in Rio de Janeiro, Brazil. The Sri Lanka MHP focused on supporting the construction of safe and legally recognised dwellings by individual urban households, so that they would benefit from the security of their houses as marketable commodities and as officially acceptable capital collateral in addition to providing convivial and healthy domestic environments. By contrast, the Favela Bairro programme did not directly address the physical upgrading of dwellings, though the granting of secure titles to property went a long way to encouraging household investment in improving dwellings, but principally aimed to improve the quality of life of urban informal settlement dwellers through the upgrading of infrastructure and urban services and the strategic targeting of social welfare programmes.

As pointed out above, the very different objectives and operational approaches to their implementation occasioned different outcomes. However, both programmes demonstrate the nature and importance of mutual understanding between the various actors engaged in their implementation. The success of the Favela Bairro programme in many *favelas* in Rio was constrained by a lack of trust between urban the residents associations, the households that they represented and the municipal government and some of the public utility agencies that were responsible for upgrading infrastructure. This was less of a problem in the Sri Lanka MHP, largely because of the community-based process by which the CDCs were constituted and the close engagement of the NHDA with them at every stage of the programme, and its emphasis on support to the provision of improved dwellings by individual households, rather than on the wider issues of urban governance and service provision as in Favela Bairro (Riley & Wakely 2005).

In neither case did the participatory upgrading initiative have a significant impact on the urban form or social structure of the city as a whole, though this was not a stated objective of the Sri Lankan MHP Urban Sub-programme, which explicitly set out to address no more than the quality of dwellings and domestic infrastructure through the provision of basic technical and minimal financial support to individual households and communities. Even in Rio, where 'the integration of the two parts of the city: 'the formal and the informal' was an important programme objective, even the most successfully improved *favelas* remained physically visible and socially distinct as low-income neighbourhoods in an otherwise wealthy city.

Nevertheless, both programmes demonstrated that decentralised public sector support to the initiatives and endeavours of poor urban households and communities could be 'taken to scale', rather than remaining at the level of isolated 'demonstration' or 'pilot' projects, and make a significant positive impact on lives and livelihoods and therefore, by extension, on the development of the city as a whole.

The OHSIP demonstrated the delicacy of introducing and sustaining novel participatory approaches to local development in a situation of political immaturity and change. At the same time showing that such conditions can support significant and deep-seated institutional innovation, despite the fragility.

Most urban low-income community organisations only come together in an organised way in response to particular crises or opportunities that are recognised by the community at large. Thus they tend to be transitory, short-lived and opportunistic, not stable, long-term, established, bodies that voluntarily take responsibility for issues of local governance or the routines of local environmental management, as do many traditional rural village councils, governed by time-honoured social hierarchies and historically embedded cultural norms, as is often erroneously assumed by urban social policy-makers. This is born out by all three cases, despite their differences, reinforcing the importance of support to building local agency capacity (e.g. principles and skills of local governance; negotiating skills; management skills; the understanding/appreciation of official administrative procedures etc.). This was a very successful aspect of the Urban Sub-programme of the Sri Lanka MHP; a decade after the closure of the programme in Colombo, CDCs that had been 'operationally dormant' since the 1980s were able to be reconstituted and operational again in the early 2000s (Redwood & Wakely 2012).

Notes

1 Over 2.2 per cent per annum between 1953 and 1971, according to Department of Census and Statistics of Sri Lanka.
2 Coalition government led by the democratic socialist Sri Lanka Freedom Party (SLFP).

3 In 2000, more than half the population of Colombo lived in informal neigh-bourhoods, locally termed 'under-served settlements'. These were customarily classified in two broad, categories: 1) <u>slums</u>: very small, old and overcrowded inner-city rental tenements, of decaying permanent construction with minimal common water supply and sanitation, known as 'tenement gardens' or subdi-vided old large houses (c. 25,500 dwellings in c. 1,070 settlements in 2007); and 2) <u>shanties</u>, generally of impermanent building materials with inadequate access to communal services and usually with no legal right to land i.e. squatters (c. 13,300 housing units in c. 183 informal settlements in 2007).

4 The MHP implementation training programme was supported with special-ist inputs by the Development Planning Unit (DPU), University College London and the SIGUS (Special Interest Group in Urban Settlement) Program, Massachusetts Institute of Technology, USA

5 Loans for building or upgrading individual houses were disbursed incrementally, starting with the cost of foundations and floor slab, on completion of which (certi-fied by a housing officer) a second loan to cover the cost of structural walls and/or columns and beams was awarded, followed by a roof loan and a loan for window and door shutters and approved finishes; all to a maximum of Rs15,000 (US$555) at 3–10 per cent interest, initially over 15 years. Loans for providing or upgrad-ing neighbourhood infrastructure were managed directly by the NHDA District Office, though the supervision of work was generally devolved to the CDC, which could (was encouraged to) undertake the work through a 'community contract'.

6 In the decade 1950–60, whilst Rio's population grew by almost 40 per cent, its *favela* population nearly doubled (Riley & Wakely 2005).

7 FAMERJ (Federação das Associações de Moradores do Estado do Rio de Janeiro – Federation of Residents Associations of the State of Rio de Janeiro) was established in 1977.

8 Companhia Estadual de Águas e Esgotos (CEDAE).

9 Secretaria Municipal de Urbanismo (SMU)

10 Secretaria Municipal de Habitação (SMH)

11 In 1994, medium-sized *favelas* (500–2,500 households) accommodated almost 60 per cent of the city's total *favela* population of more than 1 million people, the remaining c.40 per cent being distributed between small *favelas* with less than 500 households and large ones, some of which had populations of over 100,000 people.

12 Secretaria Municipal de Cultura (SMC); Secretaria Municipal de Desenvolvimento Social (SMDS); Secretaria Municipal de Educação (SME); Secretaria Municipal de Trabalho (SMTb).

13 The Republic of Namibia (formally South West Africa) gained independence from South Africa in 1990 after a 15-year war of independence against South African military forces, establishing a multi-party democracy led by SWAPO (South West Africa People's Organisation) that had been the political wing of the People's Liberation Army of Namibia (PLAN).

14 Ibis, was a leftist NGDO, dedicated to supporting freedom struggles and inde-pendence movements in colonised countries and assisting newly independent countries to establish democratic governance and effective institutions. It assem-bled a team of European professionals (an architect, a civil engineer and a social development expert), all with some experience of working in Southern Africa) to implement the project in partnership with the OTC.

15 The UNCHS chief technical adviser to the ministry was previously assistant general manager of the Sri Lanka NHDA, responsible for the MHP Urban Sub-programme.

16 Community development committees, supported by community advisors, officers of the regional Directorate of Community Development, had been established in several informal settlements in 1991 to administer welfare relief to poor households affected by a period of extreme drought throughout the region.

17 SWAPO (South West Africa Peoples Organization), the National ruling political party, headed by Sam Njoma, President of the Republic of Namibia.

18 Whilst this process was sufficiently binding to satisfy local demands for security of tenure, it did not meet the technical or procedural requirements of Government Surveyor General's Office, but it did provide a procedural precedent that generated sufficient interest for the government to consider it as an 'interim land registration' process to be applied nationally in all urban informal, and traditional, settlements.

19 '*Okakedi*' was derived from an acronym meaning 'non-smelling' in Oshiwambo.

20 A custom rapidly developed by which on the night that the streetlight was switched on in any locality, a spontaneous all-night party would get under way under the lampposts with food, beer and schnapps, loud music and dancing. Old people and school children would sit reading newspapers and books.

References

Fiori, J. & J. Brandao, 2012, 'Spatial strategies and urban social policy: Urbanism and poverty reduction in the favelas of Rio de Janeiro', in Hernandez, F., L. Allen & P. Kellett (eds) *Rethinking the Informal City: Critical Perspectives from Latin America*, Berghahn Books, Oxford, UK and New York, USA.

Fiori, J, E. Riley & R. Ramirez, 2001, 'Physical upgrading and social integration in Rio de Janeiro: The case of Favela Bairro', *DISP The Planning Review*, No. 147, Zurich, Switzerland.

Hamdi, N. & R. Goethert, 1997, *Action Planning for Cities: A Guide to Community Practice*, John Ailey & Sons, Chichester, UK.

Lankatilleke, L., 1986, 'Training and information for institutional development for the implementation of the Million Houses Programme of Sri Lanka', *Habitat International*, Vol. 10, No. 3, Pergamon Press, Oxford, UK.

Magalhães, S., 1997, Pobreza Urbana: Un fenómeno de la exclusion: La experiencia de Rio de Janeiro y el Programa Favela Bairro, Secretaria Municipal de Habitação, Rio de Janeiro, Brazil.

Ramirez, R., 2002, *Urban Poverty Reduction and Urban Security Consolidation: A New Paradigm at Work? A Review of Theory and Practice*, UN-Habitat/UNDP/World Bank Urban Management Programme (UMP) Working Paper Series No.20, Nairobi, Kenya.

Redwood, M. & P. Wakely, 2012, 'Land tenure and upgrading informal settlements in Colombo, Sri Lanka', *International Journal of Urban Sustainable Development*, Vol. 4, No. 20, Taylor &Francis, London, UK.

Riley, E. & P. Wakely, 2005, *Communities and Communication: Building Urban Partnerships*, ITDG Publishing, Rugby, UK.

Sirivardana, S., 1986, 'Reflections on the implementation of the Million Houses Programme', *Habitat International*, Vol. 10, No. 3, Pergamon, Oxford, UK.

Weerapana, D., 1986, 'Evolution of a support policy of shelter: The experience of Sri Lanka', *Habitat International*, Vol. 10, No. 3, Pergamon, Oxford, UK.

5 The Return to 'Conventional' Public Housing Provision and Incentives to Private Sector Developers

The last decades of the twentieth century saw a distinctive change in paradigm, away from 'non-conventional' participatory approaches to low-income housing production and the re-emergence of government-sponsored and/or government-built public housing for urban low-income groups. As pointed out in Chapter 2, in the 1970s-1980s, when the 'non-conventional' paradigm (sites and services (S&S) and slum upgrading) was adopted as the preferred policy option for urban low-income group housing procurement, many government housing authorities continued to undertake or sub-contract the construction of 'conventional' ready-built public housing for rent and/or sale at subsidised rates to low-income households, in many instances only on a relatively small scale.

In other cases, the construction of 'conventional' public housing continued to be the official strategic policy; 'non-conventional' S&S projects and slum upgrading programmes and projects being treated as 'one-off', extraordinary, interventions. Therefore, the mindset and operational systems were largely in place to revert to 'conventional' public housing provision in the 1980s and 1990s. This was frequently accompanied by new programmes for the disbursement of housing grants directly to low-income would-be homeowners in order to assist them in gaining access to the formal private sector housing market.

For instance, the South African Finance Linked Individual Subsidy Programme (FLISP), launched in 1997 as part of the national government's Integrated Residential Development Programme (IRDP) made lump-sum grants of R54,238 (US$5,000) to low-income[1] first-time-buyer or builder households, who were eligible for a commercial mortgage or housing loan (by a bank) but could not afford it or were unable to obtain acceptable collateral or guarantees, to buy or build a house in a development that was officially recognised as coming under the IRDP. In 2012 the upper limit of the eligible income category for FLISP subsidies was doubled and, as stated in a memo from the Director General of the national Department of Human Settlements (Housing Ministry):

> [In order to] standardise, streamline, align and centralise all the processes. . .of disbursing the subsidies, [the National Housing Finance Corporation and Provincial Departments of Human Settlements are mandated] to introduce a 'one-stop-shop' to work with [private sector] financial institutions and property developers to administer the implementation of the programme.
>
> (RSA 2012)

In effect, the government subsidy was redirected from the low-income groups to low-middle income earners and then switched from individual householders – the aspiring consumers of housing – to the (profit-motivated) producers of housing, real estate developers and banks. Despite their previous reluctance to engage with low-income group housing, private sector developers welcomed such contracts as they brought with them the guaranteed payment by government of the grant-funded subsidy component of the construction costs, relieving them of the risks and uncertainties of low-middle-income households having to secure credit (housing loans or mortgages) individually; this not only in South Africa, but also in similar policies in Brazil and Mexico.

Processes such as this illustrative example of South Africa, by which state support was transferred from aspiring low-income homeowners to the formal institutions that controlled and maintained the private sector market in housing as a commodity, in theory enabling them to reach down to lower, but not the very lowest, income groups, took place in many countries[2] during the late 1980s and 1990s, in which the new generation of 'conventional' housing strategies were dominated by the profit motives of private capital that excluded the lowest urban income groups and had little concern for the social impact of appropriate urban housing on its users, or for the form or amenity provided by urban agglomerations at large (Buckley et al. 2016). The 'commodification' of housing, whereby its commercial monetary exchange-value overrides its social use-value, occasioned the disproportionate rises in house prices in many cities throughout the world that have exacerbated defaults, evictions and homelessness in developing and developed countries alike (Madden & Marcuse 2016).

Studies of private sector 'conventional', developer-built, low-middle-income housing projects in Brazil and Mexico in the early years of the twenty first century demonstrated further problems created by the 'new' housing at the level of urban form and infrastructure provision and service delivery. In urban Mexico, the response to market demand for freehold ownership of individual houses, albeit on small plots of land, as opposed to apartments in larger blocks and at higher residential densities, was the construction by private sector developers of extensive relatively low-density housing estates on the peri-urban fringes of many towns and cities, in some cases several kilometres from the urban area, leading to urban sprawl (Solana Oses 2013).

Similar urban problems occurred in Brazil, where a study of the impact of the new generation of 'conventional' private housing development in the city of Recife, encouraged and supported by the federal government's Minha Casa, Minha Vida (My House, My Life) programme to construct one million dwellings, revealed that the drive for profit-maximising frequently led to under investment in urban infrastructure and service provision in new, municipally approved, low-middle-income housing developments by private sector developers and contractors (Fiori et al. 2014).

The new generation of 'conventional' housing strategies, as considered here, represents a significant shift in priorities for government support to the housing sector, giving greater emphasis to the upper end of the low-income scale, rather than to the poorest urban households or those in greatest need. They are more concerned with the impact of housing markets and the construction industry on growth in national and municipal economies than with the social role of secure housing in the alleviation and reduction of poverty, though, of course, these also can have a significant impact on productivity, economic stability and growth (Tibaijuka 2009).

Notes

1 In the income category R3,500–7,000 (US$320–645) per month, raised in 2012 to R3,500–15,000 (US$320–1,385) per month (RSA 2012).
2 For example: Mexico, Chile, Brazil and Sri Lanka, all of which had major 'non-conventional' housing policies and programmes with strong social objectives in the 1970s and 1980s.

References

Buckley, R.M., A. Kallergis & L. Wainer, 2016, Addressing the housing challenge: avoiding the Ozmandias Syndrome', *Environment & Urbanization*, Vol. 28, No. 1, London, UK

Fiori, J., H. Hinsley & L. Barth (eds), 2014, *Housing as Urbanism: Critical Reflections on the Brazilian Experience of Urban Housing*, Architectural Association, London, UK.

Madden, D. & P. Marcuse, 2016, *In Defense of Housing: The Politics of Crisis*, Verso, London, UK and New York, USA.

RSA (Republic of South Africa) Human Settlements Department, 2012, *Adjustments to the Finance Linked Individual Subsidy Programme*, un-published memo, Human Settlements Department, www.dhs.gov.za (accessed Feb. 2014), Pretoria, South Africa.

Solana Oses, O., 2013, *Affordable Housing and Urban Sprawl in Mexico: the Need for a Paradigm shift*, University of Manchester, Global Urban Research Centre, Briefing Paper No.4, Manchester, UK.

Tibaijuka, A.K., 2009, *Building Prosperity: Housing and Economic Development*, Earthscan, London, UK.

6   Where Next

Clearly the way forward lies neither exclusively in the direct construction of 'conventional' public housing nor only in government support to 'non-conventional' self-help approaches to the delivery and maintenance of housing and urban domestic infrastructure and services by low-income households and communities; nor does it lie solely in 'enabling [supply-led private sector housing] markets to work', as expounded by the World Bank's 1993 *Housing Policy* paper (World Bank 1993).

In any developing city the need for official support to the production, maintenance and management of appropriate housing and community facilities, that is fundamentally redistributive and/or committed to urban poverty alleviation and reduction, is so complex that no single strategic approach to housing production can possibly suffice equitably and effectively (Marcuse 1992).

Thus, the next generation of urban housing policies, and strategies for their implementation, must embrace a range of different programme and project approaches, principal amongst which will be support to 'non-conventional' incremental *social housing* and to the production of good quality *public housing* that provides socially controlled rental accommodation that is affordable to those households in the lowest income groups who are unable/unwilling to invest in fixed capital assets such as urban property (see Section 7.2).

A holistic approach to supporting urban low-income housing that is sensitive and responsive to the particular social, economic and political circumstances of any urban area, neighbourhood or community, and is sustainable over the medium- to long-term, embracing the principle of subsidiarity, can only be administered effectively at a level of government no higher than that of the municipality. However, as pointed out in Chapter 2, in very many countries housing policies and operational strategies for their implementation are administered by national-level authorities that rarely entertain the devolution of any real power or decision-making down to the level of local government and municipal administration, and virtually never to levels of local organisation below that (i.e. assigning officially recognised governance or administrative roles or responsibility to community-based organisations (CBOs) and/or the non-governmental organisations (NGOs) that support them).

Thus, in most countries, recognition of the principle of subsidiarity and the devolution of authority in the housing sector is an essential starting point. However, 'municipalisation' and the co-existence, not to mention the integration, of alternative policy approaches are likely to pose some fundamental political/ideological contradictions (Fiori & Ramirez 1992). It also invariably calls for radical changes in the management of urban development and the administration of urban infrastructure and service delivery that in many towns and cities require complex and often contentious processes to ensure inter-agency cooperation or collaboration.

To assist and enhance this, it is conceptually helpful to disentangle the production of dwelling units to meet politically determined production targets (the 'numbers game') from the contribution of good, safe and secure housing and domestic infrastructure to the wider social processes of equitable urban development, notably the alleviation of the social impacts of poverty, poverty reduction and enhancing the productivity of low-income urban communities and enterprises in the urban economy at large. Clearly, to be effective municipal housing policies and programmes must address all these issues simultaneously, combining 'non-conventional' participatory incremental housing production, maintenance and management with, for example, 'conventional' constructed (subsidised) public rental housing. Such an approach should also take into account and contribute to the rationalisation of the urban structure (form) of the city to ensure coherence between different areas of the city and the functions and amenities that they provide for the city as a whole as well as for those who live and/or work in them. Thus, initiating integrated and sustainable urban development, as expounded by the 2016 United Nations New Urban Agenda, for Housing and Sustainable Urban Development (Habitat III) and the UN Sustainable Development Goals (SDGs) 2015–2030[1] and embracing the goals and targets for the mitigation of climate change in and by urban areas, principally the reduction and control of greenhouse gas emissions, as agreed by the The Paris Agreement of the UN Framework Convention on Climate Change in Paris in December 2015.[2]

As pointed out at the start of this book, in physical terms, housing is a major component of all towns and cities in Asia, Africa, the Middle East, Latin America and the Caribbean, typically covering 60–80 per cent of the developed land area of towns and cities and accounting for 50–70 per cent of the value of the fixed capital formation of the urban areas of which it is an integral part (UN-Habitat 2003). Thus, low-income group housing policies and strategies for their implementation cannot be divorced from policies and strategies for the development, planning and management of towns and cities as a whole, as they have been, and still are, in many countries.

6.1 City Development Strategies

City Development Strategies (CDSs) and comprehensive urban (physical) development plans offer democratic, participatory ways into the new agenda for inclusive housing and urban development (Freire & Stren 2001; Cities Alliance 2006).

CDSs, strongly promoted by international aid agencies in the closing decades of the twentieth century, took two distinct conceptual forms: (1) those espoused by the World Bank and Cities Alliance, focusing on citywide economic development and productivity; and (2) those principally promoted and supported by United Nations agencies, notably UN-Habitat, the UN Children's Fund (UNICEF), the UN Environment Porgramme (UNEP) and the Asian and Inter-American Development Banks that gave greater emphasis to sustainable social, managerial and environmental development in cities and settlements. Whatever the focus, all CDS procedures are operationally founded on inclusive participatory principles – 'city forums' – that engage senior representatives of formal local (municipal) government and administration, private sector enterprise (e.g. chambers of commerce and industry, etc.), labour unions and other NGOs, including CBOs, thereby ensuring a significant level of buy-in and communication between, and the participation of, different interest groups and segments of the urban society and economy, both formal and informal, governmental and non-governmental.[3] The starting point of a CDS development process is the formulation of an agreed understanding of a city's characteristics (strengths, weaknesses, opportunities and threats – SWOT) and a common vision for its future. With this basis and the support of a series of technical 'task forces' (committees), city forums then debate, agree and articulate a programme of strategic actions that will, over time, work towards realising the vision. CDSs have embraced different emphases in different cities. For example in the CDS for Tunis, Tunisia gave emphasis to the safety and security of women; in Karu, the CDS Nigeria concentrated on developing the strength of the city's informal sector productivity and economy; while the Mumbai, India CDS, coordinated by the Mumbai Chamber of Commerce and Industry Mumbai First movement, sought to make Mumbai a world class city able to compete economically with Shanghai or Singapore. Clearly poverty reduction and housing, particularly for low-income groups, have featured highly in CDSs worldwide (Cities Alliance 2006).

Whatever operational approach is adopted for the development and sustained management of acceptable and affordable urban housing, it is important that it is supported by a comprehensive and sensitive understanding of the city, underpinned by a thorough and dynamic (constantly up-dated) open-access database that includes information on prevailing housing needs, demands and actual and potential resources, on the basis of which policies for public sector support can be designed and operational strategies for their implementation, can be drawn up and budgeted

6.2 Housing-need Sub-groups

It is likely that any such a city housing development strategy will embrace a set of broad householder affordability categories, for example distinguishing between:

1   *Upper-income groups* that are generally able to access acceptable housing through the private sector market, requiring little, if any, public sector support except, perhaps, the administration of incentives for the provision of mortgage finance by commercial banks, and secure access to appropriately located and serviced land;

2   *Middle-income groups*, a large proportion of which is also served by the formal private sector market, though in many countries householders need the assistance of relatively 'soft' finance or/and financial guarantee facilities. Public sector intervention in the procurement and management of housing for this and the upper-income groups also often requires rigorously enforced quality control (planning and building regulations) of developer-produced housing to ensure that adequate and appropriately located land is made available for community service and amenity facilities and recreation space and socially acceptable building and infrastructure standards, service delivery and environmental conditions[4] and to avoid uncontrolled peri-urban sprawl by unregulated private sector development, which in many cities such as Accra, Ghana, was rampant in the 1990s (Buckley et al. 2016);

3   *Lower-income groups*, aspiring to move up to middle-income status and enter the formal private sector housing market, though they do not have the resources or capacity to acquire serviced land and build houses and neighbourhood facilities. Thus, they need more rigorous/interventionist support than the middle-income group;

4   *Lowest-income groups* that, due to poverty (lack of physical, financial or social assets and security), are unable to enter the formal private sector housing market at any level and are therefore dependent upon their own informal, unregulated (illegal) housing developments that are frequently insecure, unsafe and exploitative, as discussed in Chapter 1.

Therefore they need assistance with community organisation; secure tenure to land; infrastructure and environmental upgrading; and technical assistance and financial support for house building and improvement. A large proportion of this group in many cities, who are unable or unwilling to invest in urban real estate, occupy rental housing;

5 *Rental housing.* Government sponsored incentives for private sector developers and landlords, including 'subsistence landlords' (Kumar 2011), are often needed to provide acceptable, rental accommodation that is affordable to the lowest income group households. Public sector constructed 'conventional' rental housing, located and designed in collaboration with representatives of its eventual low-income group occupants and users, is also appropriate in this category, as discussed in Section 7.2.

6.3 Cultural Integration and Cosmopolitan Development

In some cities further categories or sub-categories of this broad classification by income group and affordability, such as clearly identifiable cultural, ethnic or social groups that require special social considerations or facilities, such as land for particular religious and cultural buildings or celebrations, may have to be included in urban development and housing policies and operational strategies for their implementation. The identification of such sub-groups and responses to their particular local needs are political processes, peculiar to every neighbourhood and city, and cannot be generalised. However, cases of sensitive 'cosmopolitan planning' and development do provide examples, from which useful principles and practices to assist the identification of different social and cultural housing support need groups and strategic planning approaches to them, can be drawn, giving emphasis to fostering ethnic, religious and cultural harmony and conviviality (e.g. Beall et al. 2002).

Whilst it is important that such categorisation is included in city databases to facilitate citywide programme planning and budgeting, there is a danger of it becoming the driver of project-level planning by municipal housing authorities, which should be avoided, as it is likely to induce top-down, historically determined social divisions that can lead to involuntary 'ghettoisation' and ultimately to civil strife. Such a degree of segregation can effectively only be made voluntarily, at a community-level, provided that an appropriate and capable institutional capacity exists, such as the Community Development Councils in Colombo, Sri Lanka and the *favela* residents associations in Rio de Janeiro, Brazil, discussed in Chapter 4. Inevitably, there will be divisions and disputes, possibly between majority and minority interest groups in any neighbourhood-wide community organisation. Municipal or metropolitan housing authorities should establish a widely (Riley & Wakely 2005) respected impartial arbitration capacity to address such disputes at the local level.

The first decades of the twenty-first century saw dramatic and tragic increase in the migration to cities of refugees and internally displaced persons (IDPs) from political and civil strife and 'natural' disasters. In response the UN New Urban Agenda (UN-Habitat 2016) expressly commits city administrations to 'respect the rights of refugees, migrants and internally displaced persons, regardless of their migration status'.[5] requiring special consideration in the housing policies and implementation strategies of cities and other urban areas in many countries.

6.4 Gender Needs and Assets

It is essential that the different gender needs of men and women are recognised and responded to at all levels and in all fields of strategic planning and resource allocation. In nearly all developing urban societies built on historical patriarchal traditions, emphasis in the access to housing has been given to men on the assumption that they are the heads of households, family breadwinners and the owners and principal users of property. Almost universally, however, women are in fact the main users and managers of domestic property, in which they feed and maintain households, including the nurturing of children, and often undertake income-earning activities that augment overall household financial resources. The lack of recognition of women's roles and the inadequate allocation of moral, social and physical resources to maintain them seriously imbalances the access to housing assets that constitute the predominant, if not the only, source of social and financial security available to urban low-income families (Moser 2016). Furthermore, in many cities women are further discriminated against by legislation and administrative procedures that militate against, or totally negate, their security of tenure to housing and urban property[6] (Rakodi 2016). Such discriminatory measures have had a particularly severe impact on women-headed households, the global incidence of which grew significantly in the closing decades of the twentieth century (Chant 2013).

Attempts to redress the gender-based inequities in access to secure urban housing have included one-off project- and programme-level approaches such as the issue of title deeds for public housing only in the name of women household members.[7] Whilst such 'special-case' pragmatic (top-down) approaches can benefit the individual women involved, not only in securing adequate and appropriate shelter, but also the social standing and financial security that it provides, such one-off strategies do little to create sustainable structural transformation out of gender-based inequalities in access to urban housing.

The Platform for Action (PfA) that emerged from the fourth UN World Women's Conference on Action for Equality, Development and Peace in Beijing, China, in 1995 was a universally endorsed agenda for women's empowerment.[8] Amongst other achievements, it saw a significant increase in NGO activity in support of women's rights and their political engagement in housing and urban development.

For instance, in Ghana in the early 2000s the NGO Ashaiman Women for Progressive Development (AWPD), with support from the Danish non-governmental development organisation (NGDO) Ibis, developed from a women's education and social support grouping in the large, multi-ethnic informal settlement of Ashaiman in the city of Tema,[9] into a strong political force, including popularly elected Tema Metropolitan Assembly members with a powerful lobby for good housing, environmental health and sanitation in the city as a whole as well as in Ashaiman. The political success of the AWPD drew media attention to the structural disparities between men and women in local governance in Ghana and to the need for institutional change to address them.

The Sri Lanka Women's Bank, the origins and operation of which were firmly based on empowering women through their control over financial resources for the production and improvement of housing and domestic infrastructure, discussed at some length in Section 4.1, attests to the effectiveness of 'bottom-up' housing-related savings-and-loans schemes and cooperative banking by and for women as a means to their empowerment through a measure of financial independence and control over their domestic environment. The saving of (small) sums of money by women as a regular discipline is a mainstay of women's empowerment and community development of the NGO coalition of Society for the Promotion of Area Resource Centres (SPARC), National Slum Dwellers Federation (NSDF) and Mahila Milan[10] in India (Patel & Mitlin 2004) that has been adopted as an operating principle of Shack/Slum Dwellers International (SDI).

However such bottom-up 'empowerment' strategies, important and effective as they are, are not sufficient to redress the gender imbalance in access to, and the management of, housing in the many countries in which public housing policy, legislation and procedures discriminate heavily against women. Repealing and recasting many such procedures is likely to entail institutional changes at a national level (see Section 9.1) and embrace institutional transformations in gender policies on a wider front than the remit of low-income group urban housing, as has been achieved in the Republic of South Africa since democratisation in1994, and in Peru, through its Equal Opportunities Act of 2007 (Moser 2017).

6.5 Climate Change and Geophysical Hazards

The early decades of the twenty-first century have seen the dramatic and tragic impacts of global climate change, particularly on low-income group settlements. Whilst strategies to minimise the severity of the extremes of the world's climates, notably as the result of global warming through the emission of 'greenhouse' gases,[11] have been addressed politically by international bodies and agreements, with varying degrees of success,[12] it seems extremely unlikely that any international political or technical innovations will reduce the vulnerability of urban settlements to the impacts of global climate change before the end of this century, but they can be mitigated by informed planning for enhanced resilience to hazards, thereby reducing risks of disaster[13] from extreme climatic conditions such as flooding and drought, storms and high winds, and geophysical hazards such as earthquakes, tsunamis and landslides (UN-Habitat 2011).

The impact of climate change hazards, such as seasonal rains that have occasional unpredictable extremes, should be mitigated by judicious planning and infrastructure engineering that take into account seasonal occurrences and the possibility of unexpected peaks, without radically increasing the capital cost or maintenance expenditure in use. Long-term environmental changes, such as sea-level rise, or extended periods of drought and/or extreme air temperature increases (heat waves), can be addressed by informed good planning and design practice. In many regions long-term climate change can have significant effects at a regional level that impact directly upon urban low-income housing. For instance, sustained periods of drought or extensive flooding can disrupt agricultural production in rural areas, occasioning increased migration to towns and cities by ex-farmers seeking shelter and employment in urban low-income group (informal) settlements.

Local government administrations in towns and cities in regions prone to geophysical hazards, such as earthquakes, landslides and tsunamis are aware of the potential for disaster and in most cases include mitigation measures in their planning and building procedures and legislation (World Bank 2015). However, urban low-income group housing areas and informal settlements frequently are not protected by such official safety measures, rendering them the most prone to disasters. In these situations, therefore, there is a need to ensure that appropriate precautions are taken in the location and planning of areas designated for low-income group incremental housing development, and that appropriate advice and technical support is given to the design and construction of dwellings and community buildings and also to the provision of such measures as safe escape routes and buildings of permanent construction such as community centres and schools that can act as storm shelters in the case of flooding by surge tides, tsunamis and cyclones in coastal towns and cities. It is important that such measures are designed and implemented by local authorities in close collaboration with the communities that are in potential danger, and also that reliable communication and early-warning procedures are in place and well understood at all levels of local administration, including that of community based organisations.

In the immediate wake of the 2004 Asian tsunami, the government of Sri Lanka declared all coastal land, within 100–200 metres from the mean high water line an interim nationwide coastal buffer zone, in which it was prohibited to construct or repair any buildings, regardless of its coast-line topography or whether it was urban or rural. The interim buffer zone served the purpose of obviating any *ad hoc* opportunistic, land grabbing and unauthorised (unsafe) development in the inevitably chaotic immedi-ate aftermath of the tragedy, but soon had to be replaced by a more locally specific set of measures that also embraced the ecological conservation of the fragile natural coastal environment. In urban areas new environmental safety measures were drawn up by local authorities in conjunction with the national Urban Development Authority and the participation of local private sector institutions, NGOs and CBOs. These were then incorporated in the relevant planning and building bylaws, governing all seafront development, including low-income group housing and enterprises, mostly occupied by fishermen and other sea-dependent trades.

The lessons leant from the Sri Lankan example for the mitigation of risk from coastal threats apply equally to other geophysical hazards and those originating from extreme climatic occurrences such as riparian flooding caused by storms, hurricanes and cyclones or glacial melt water from unu-sually high temperatures in mountainous regions that my be a considerable distance from the urban area of impact. Such occurrences are not uncom-mon in parts of the Andes.

As well as causing hazards from surface run-off flooding, heavy and persistent rainfall can cause ground water saturation that can precipitate landslides in steeply inclined topography, which, in many cities are the sites of informal settlements where the lowest-income group households live and work (see Figure 1.4 on p. 5 and Figures 4.4 and 4.5 on p. 73).

Conditions of severe drought, as experienced in East Africa in 2017, occasioned by acute and sustained rise in air temperature (heat wave), com-pounded by the failure of seasonal rainfall, can have a disastrous impact on water supplies at a regional level, affecting urban and rural communities alike.[14] There are no particular risks from periods of drought that distin-guish urban low-income group neighbourhoods and communities as more vulnerable than the rest of the city except their poverty and customary lack of access to the decision-making power structures that control the distribu-tion of resources, such as potable water. Hence the importance of recasting urban decision-making and managerial structures for low-income groups as outlined in Chapter 7, below.

Building research has established norms and standards for earthquake-proof construction that are available internationally and are incorporated in building codes and regulations in earthquake-prone regions universally

(World Bank 2015). It is very important that good safety practices and techniques for neighbourhood planning and the construction of dwellings are conveyed as part of the technical support to incremental housing development processes in locations that are prone to earthquakes and other geophysical hazards. In many parts of the world, experience has shown that traditional, indigenous construction practices often result in buildings that are resistant to such hazards, even when transferred to the construction of urban housing. For instance, it was found that buildings constructed of local materials using traditional building methods – wattle-and-daub, bamboo and timber – withstood the 2010 Haiti earthquake in Port-au-Prince and other towns better than many 'modern' buildings that collapsed, with heavy loss of life and injury (Audefroy 2011). However, traditional (rural) construction in many cities is classified as 'impermanent' and disallowed in municipal building bylaws.

The latter half of the twentieth century and the first decades of the twenty-first century demonstrated the impressive capacity of governments and international aid efforts to provide financial and technical emergency support to the first stages of recovery from geophysical disasters.[15] Important though the initial emergency assistance is, once it is exhausted and the aid workers leave the scene of disaster, the affected families and enterprises are often left to recover and remake their lives on their own, unaided. There has been a move to draw attention to the importance of supporting the processes of initiating and sustaining the medium- to long-term development of the livelihoods, economies and environments of people and communities who have suffered the trauma of disaster (Lloyd-Jones 2006). By taking this a step even further than the slogan 'build back better',[16] the social and physical trauma of a disaster can be perceived as a catalyst for change and development. It gets people and communities 'out of the rut' of every-day habits and obligations, enabling them to look ahead with greater ambition and courage than they could previously muster. For example, many of the survivors of Cyclone Nagris in Myanmar in 2008 persuaded aid donor agencies to give their aid as cash grants, rather than to rebuild their houses and physical infrastructure for them. This they used to establish new settlements and new enterprises as the start to a new life ahead, with considerable success that was internationally acclaimed (Archer & Boonyabancha 2011).

In summary, low-income households and communities are more prone to the impacts of climate change and geophysical hazards than higher urban income groups due to poverty that tends to force them to inhabit the most vulnerable locations and because their economic and locational circumstances have been overlooked or not given sufficient consideration in the administration of risk-mitigating development control measures. Where disaster has struck, there is significant evidence that, when appropriate support has been provided to enable low-income group households and communities to manage their own recovery and reconstruction of their neighbourhoods and dwellings, a platform has often been created from which further, long-term development can take off, to the benefit of disaster survivors and the wider urban community at large.

6.6 Energy Conservation and Environmental Sustainability

The production and maintenance of urban housing and domestic infrastructure of all classes has been a major consumer of energy that almost universally has been generated by the consumption of non-renewable, finite natural sources.

The UN World Commission on Environment and Development (WCED) commonly known as the Bruntland Commission,[17] convened in 1983, published its report on sustainable development entitled, *Our Common Future* in 1987.[18] This, together with the outcome of the United Nations Conference on Environment and Development (UNCED), the Earth Summit held in Rio de Janeiro, Brazil in 1992 – the Rio Declaration on Environment and Development, Agenda 21[19] – brought the attention of governments to their dependence on natural resources for the usable supply of energy, notably oil, coal, combustible natural gas and forest products, and the rate at which they were being depleted, threatening the global environment and the very existence of humanity and all other forms of life on earth, and calling for fundamental changes in the prevailing economic and development paradigms (Atkinson 2009).

The predominant concerns of urban energy conservation and environmental sustainability fall into two broad sets of issues: the 'Green' and 'Brown' Agendas:

- *The Green Agenda* is principally concerned with macro-scale depletion of natural resources occasioned by their profligate use as fuel for the generation of energy, notably electricity, industrial production, building construction, motor transport, etc.
- *The Brown Agenda* refers to stemming the deterioration of the quality of local urban environmental conditions, such as air pollution, sanitation/ sewerage and solid waste disposal; also the generation of pollutants and greenhouse gases that may have a wider regional or global impact ('footprint') than the geographic confines of the city (see Section 6.5).

The Brown Agenda largely addresses issues that are traditionally and correctly managed at the local (project) level, entailing no less nor more than good urban development planning and housing policy implementation and management practices, as discussed in Chapter 8. The urban Green Agenda for energy conservation and environmental sustainability embraces the conservation of energy and natural resources through the management of processes of both the production and consumption of goods and services, including housing and domestic infrastructure. In many countries these require legislative and administrative action at the city, national or regional level as well as operational controls at the local level, for example on technical issues of housing construction[20] and domestic energy consumption,

Perhaps the most publicised of such problems is that of the private automobile, now well understood to be a major contributor to urban environmental degradation through air pollution and carbon monoxide emission and the abundant consumption of fossil fuels, especially petroleum. However in many low-density cities, private motor vehicles are the only practicable means of transport (Atkinson 2009). This and other energy-consuming urban services and infrastructure, such as street lighting, call for the need for greater attention to urban form and the need for compact cities, rather than low-density suburban extensions that, as discussed in Chapter 5, proliferated towards the end of the twentieth century (Jenks & Burgess 2000).

Any efficient, equitable and sustainable approach to the production, maintenance and management of urban housing, however, must simultaneously embrace both the Green and Brown Agendas (Allen & You 2002). For example the Republic of Cyprus, an island state with no indigenous fossil fuel resources and therefore heavily dependent on international imports, in the last decades of the twentieth century invested in an energy policy based on renewable sources, notably solar energy, such that by the end of the century, over 90 per cent of all urban and rural dwellings were fitted with solar collectors,[21] generating a total of c. 350,000 megawatts/year and reducing the nation's carbon dioxide emissions by some 10 per cent, whilst providing domestic energy at virtually no cost to the consumer-households.

Many other examples of integrating the roles of macro and micro levels of authority and action in the linking the Green and Brown Agendas and the production and maintenance of affordable housing exist, such as community-managed solid waste and recycling administered by the Santo André Municipal Environmental Sanitation Department in Greater São Paulo, Brazil, and the long-term, comprehensive, integrated Sustainable Chennai Project in India that demonstrate multiple ways in which local action can effectively address the challenges of environmentally sustainable housing and urban development, whilst conserving global energy sources (see Allen & You 2002; Wakely & You 2001).

Thus, despite the apparent reduction of public sector support to local community and individual initiatives in the production, maintenance and management of housing by the lowest urban income groups in many developing countries at the end of the twentieth century, largely as a result of a lack of understanding of pertinent criteria for the evaluation of sites and services (S&S) projects, as outlined in Section 3.4, strong arguments for government support to locally managed social housing strategies remain relevant in most developing towns and cities, as stipulated by the UN New Urban Agenda of 2016 (UN-Habitat 2016).

Also, despite the failure of and widespread abandonment of 'conventional' public housing production in the 1980s, discussed in Chapter 2, there is a case to be made in many cities for the production of ready-built (subsidised) rental housing for the lowest urban income groups, who cannot, or do not want to, invest in formal freehold home ownership. However, as will be argued in Section 7.2, unlike earlier 'conventional' public housing provision, its production, maintenance and management should be undertaken by, or in partnership with, organised community groups of (potential) tenants. To the extent possible, such public rental housing should be provided in small infill clusters in close proximity to other areas of low-income

Figure 6.1 Gothamipura, Colombo, Sri Lanka (2016). Four-storey blocks of rental flats (16 small, two-roomed flats per block), built by the NHDA on the edge of Gothamipura informal settlement, managed by Residents Committees and NHDA in collaboration with Gothamipura Community Development Councils (CDCs). The freehold titles of several flats were bought by the occupants a few years after occupation. (Photo: K.A.Jayaratne)

group housing, not in large homogeneous estates, as has been common in the past. This will foster social cohesion and the integration of public housing tenants in local informal governance and neighbourhood environmental management structures. Such a strategy has been successfully implemented by the Sri Lanka National Housing Development Authority (NHDA) in Colombo.

Notes

1 Notably SDG Goal 11 to 'Make cities and human settlements inclusive, safe, resilient and sustainable', Target 1 of which is, 'By 2030, ensure access for all to adequate, safe and affordable housing and basic services, and upgrade slums'.
2 See *Nature* magazine, UK, October 2016.
3 See also: UN-Habitat/United Nations Development Programme/World Bank Urban Management Programme 1989–2006 City Consultations, which had identical objectives and similar procedures to CDSs.
4 Also, depending on location and local conditions, land for public use by a wider population than the immediate neighbourhood, thereby assisting the integration of new urban areas in the broader fabric of the city.
5 In 2016 the United Nations High Commission for Refugees (UNHCR) reported that 'over 60 percent of the world's 19.5 million refugees, and 80 percent of the world's 34 million internally displaced, live in urban areas. More than 7 of every 10 people displaced across or within international borders seek safety and futures in cities'.
6 Legislation related to definitions of 'head of household', 'entitlement to inheritance of property'; registration and property tax procedures, etc.
7 In many instances this was more to do with the perception that women were more efficient and reliable household (financial) managers than men, thereby representing a lower risk of default in loan repayments, than to do with explicitly empowering women, though of course it also did.
8 Embracing a 'full and equal share in economic, social, cultural and political decision-making in all spheres of public and private life'.
9 At that stage the informal settlement of Ashaiman was one of five zonal councils in the Tema Metropolitan Assembly area. Subsequently, because of its size (population 300,000) and good local governance, it was upgraded to a municipality in its own right.
10 Mahila Milan means Women Together.
11 Water vapour, carbon dioxide, methane, nitrous oxide, ozone, fluorocarbons, of which industrially emitted carbon dioxide (CO_2) has the greatest negative impact.
12 See the proceedings of the UN Intergovernmental Panel on Climate Change (IPCC) and the reports of the UN International Framework Convention on Climate Change (UNFCCC) and the various international conferences and subsidiary body meetings, the Kyoto Protocol 1997 and the Paris Accord 2015.
13 The Centre for Research on the Epidemiology of Disasters (CRED) defines disaster as 'a situation or event, which overwhelms local capacity (10 or more people killed; 100 people affected; loss and/or significant damage to property)'.
14 It is estimated that 'by 2050 as many as 350–600 million people in Africa could be affected by drought' (UN-Habitat 2011).

15 Examples according to the CRED EM-DAT Database (quoted in Lloyd-Jones 2006) include:

Earthquake, Iran, 2003 (26,796 dead; 45,000 homeless; US$1 billion damage).

Earthquake, Morocco, 2004 (628 dead; 12,539 homeless; US$400 million damage).

Flooding, Bangladesh, 2004 (1,630 dead; 69,000,000 affected; US$2.42 billion damage).

Tsunami, South and South-East Asia, 2004 (223,492 dead; 400,000 homeless; US$10 billion damage).

Flooding, Pakistan, 2005 (520 dead; 7 million affected).

Hurricane Dennis, Cuba, 2005 (16 dead; 2.5 million affected; US$1.4 million damage).

Hurricane Katrina, USA, 2005 (1,322 dead; 500,000 affected; US$1.25 billion damage).

Earthquake, Pakistan, 2005 (73,338 dead; 2.8 million homeless; US$5 billion damage)

Cyclone Nagris, Myanmar, 2008 (138,366 dead; US$10 billion damage)

16 First coined by UNICEF in reference to international relief and recovery efforts following the South and Sout-East Asian tsunami, 2004–05.

17 Named after its after its chairperson, Gro Harlem Bruntland, former prime minister of Norway.

18 The Bruntland Report was made famous by defining 'sustainable development' as: 'development that meets the needs of the present without compromising the ability of future generations to meet their own needs'.

19 'An action Agenda for the 21st Century' for the UN, other multilateral organisations, and individual governments around the world to be executed at local, national, and global levels. Agenda 21 and its subsidiary report, Local Agenda 21, were popularised by the dictum: 'Think globally and act locally'.

20 For instance, promotion of the use of building materials from renewable (or recycled) and indigenous sources and limiting those that consume extensive energy in their production or transport, such as the extensive use of steel or cement, the production of which also generates high levels of atmospheric pollution, as do polycarbonate materials that release excessive greenhouse gases into the earth's atmosphere.

21 Domestic solar collector panels were fabricated in the country (using imported aluminium, the smelting of which will have consumed a relatively large amount of energy – probably generated by non-renewable sources and emitting atmospheric pollutants). The domestic solar panels could be installed at a cost of c. 700 euros per dwelling, for which government subsidies were provided.

References

Allen, A. & N. You (eds), 2002, *Sustainable Urbanisation: Bridging the Green and Brown Agendas*, Development Planning Unit (DPU), University College London (UCL), London, UK.

Archer, D. & S. Boonyabancha, 2011, 'Seeing a disaster as an opportunity: Harnessing the energy of disaster survivors for change', *Environment & Urbanization*, Vol. 23,No. 2, Sage, London, UK.

Atkinson, A., 2009, 'Climate change policy, energy and cities', *International Journal of Urban Sustainable Development*, Vol. 1, Nos. 1–2, Taylor and Francis, Abingdon, UK & New York, USA

Audefroy, J.F., 2011, 'Haiti: Post earthquake lessons learned from traditional construction', *Environment & Urbanization*, Vol. 23.No. 2, Sage, London, UK.

Beall, J., O. Crankshaw & S. Parnell, 2002, *Uniting a Divided City: Governance and Social Exclusion in Johannasburg*, Earthscan, London, UK.

Chant, S., 2013, 'Cities through a "gender lens": a golden 'urban age' for women in the Global South', *Environment & Urbanization*, Vol. 25, No. 1, Sage, London, UK.

Buckley, R.M., A. Kallergis & L. Wainer, 2016, 'Addressing the housing challenge: Avoiding the Ozmandias Syndrome', *Environment & Urbanization*, Vol. 28, No. 1, London, UK.

Cities Alliance, 2006, *Guide to City Development Strategies: Improving Urban Performance*, Cities Alliance, Washington DC, USA.

Freire, M. & R. Stren (eds), 2001, *The Challenge of Urban Government: Polices and Practices*, World Bank Institute Development Studies, Washington DC, USA

Fiori, J. & R. Ramirez, 1992, 'Notes on the Self-Help Housing Critique' in Mathéy, K. (ed)., *Beyond Self-Help Housing* , Mansell, London, U.K.

Jenks, M. & R. Burgess (eds), 2000, *Compact Cities. Sustainable Urban Forms for Developing Countries*, Spon Press, London, UK.

Kumar, S., 2011, 'The research–policy dialectic: A critical reflection on the virility of landlord–tenant research and the impotence of rental housing policy formulation in the urban Global South', *City*, Vol. 15, No. 6, London, UK.

Lloyd-Jones, T., 2006, *Mind the Gap! Post-disaster Reconstruction and the Transition from Humanitarian Relief*, Max Lock Centre, University of Westminster/RICS, London, UK.

Marcuse, P., 1992, 'Why conventional self-help projects won't work', in Mathéy, K. (ed.), *Beyond Self-Help Housing*, Mansell, London, U.K.

Moser, C.O.N., 2016, 'Towards a nexus linking gender assets and transformational pathways in just cities', in Moser, C.O.N, (ed.) *Gender, Asset Accumulation and Just Cities: Pathways to Transformation*, Routledge, Abingdon, UK & New York, USA.

Moser, C.O.N., 2017, 'Gender transformation in a new global urban agenda: Challenges for Habitat III and Beyond', *Environment & Urbanization*, Vol. 29, No. 1, Sage, London, UK.

Patel, S. & D. Mitlin, 2004, 'The work of SPARC, The National Slum Dwellers Federation and Mahila Milan', in Mitlin, D. & D. Satterthwaite (eds) *Empowering Squatter Citizens: The Roles of Local Governments and Civil Society in Reducing Urban Poverty*, Earthscan, London, UK.

Rakodi, C., 2016, 'Addressing gendered inequalities in access to land and housing', in Moser, C.O.N. (ed.), *Gender, Asset Accumulation and Just Cities: Pathways to Transformation*, Routledge, Abingdon, UK & New York, USA.

Riley, E. & P. Wakely, 2005 *'Communities and Communication: Building Urban Partnerships'* ITDG Publishing, Rugby, UK.

UN-Habitat, 2003, *The Challenge of Slums: Global Report on Human Settlements 2003*, (revised 2010), Earthscan, London, UK.

UN-Habitat, 2011, *Cities and Climate Change: Global Report on Human Settlements 2011*, Earthscan, London, UK.

UN-Habitat, 2016, *Habitat III New Urban Agenda*. Online at: http://habitat3.org/wp-content/uploads/N1639668-English.pdf.

Wakely, P. & N. You, (eds) 2001, *Implementing the Habitat Agenda: In Search of Urban Sustainability*, Development Planning Unit (DPU), University College London (UCL), London, UK.

World Bank, 1993, *Housing: Enabling Markets to Work*, World Bank Policy Paper, Washington DC, USA.

World Bank, 2015, *Building Regulation for Resilience: Managing Risks for Safer Cities*, World Bank, Washington DC, USA.

World Commission on Environment & Development, 1987, *Our Common Future (The Bruntland Report)*, Oxford University Press, Oxford, UK.

7 Partnership Paradigm for the Twenty-first Century

The new 'partnership' paradigm that is emerging for state intervention in urban housing production, maintenance and management in the twenty-first century is a holistic combination of the most equitable, efficient and sustainable aspects and components drawn from the range of approaches and lessons learnt from experience over the preceding half century – none radically new, but all substantially changed. The fundamental operational characteristics of the new paradigm are:

1) *the principle of subsidiarity* – the recognition and devolution of responsibility to the most effective level of decision-making and authority;
2) *the engagement of all stakeholders* in the formation of public-private sector partnerships that embrace local (metropolitan and municipal) government, formal and informal private sector institutions and voluntary organisations, non-governmental organisations (NGOs) and federations of community-based organisations (CBOs) (Riley & Wakely 2005); and
3) the recognition that the procurement of socially acceptable housing by any urban income or social group is a *long-term, incremental process*[1] that, for the lowest urban income groups, typically entails the construction and improvement of dwellings and, in some cases, neighbourhood infrastructure, by stages that may take many months or years to complete.

Partnership is a voluntary agreement to collaborate in order to reach mutually respected aims, sharing both the risks and benefits of actions and activities undertaken jointly or separately,[2] in this case to procure, manage and maintain socially acceptable, affordable housing that is sustainable over the long term.

Equitable partnerships are based on mutual trust and understanding of the goals, objectives and aspirations of all partners, by all partners (i.e. government authorities and agencies and (aspirant) housing-related community organisations and individual households). They therefore depend on high levels of explicit transparency and inter-stakeholder communication (Riley & Wakely 2005). They differ significantly from other, more common, contractual arrangements and legally determined obligations that are controlled by financial sanctions and imposed authoritarian actions, such as eviction and/or confiscation of property that have, explicitly or implicitly, underpinned many supposedly participatory public housing programmes and projects in the past, frequently erroneously termed 'partnerships'.

Of course, authentic partnerships are not just casual, informal, agreements; they must be backed by clear legal 'articles of association' that spell out the obligations, roles and relationships of each partner organisation. At the level of project implementation, there are likely to be further, particular, legally binding, contractual commitments to be entered into separately by each partner, particularly CBOs.

Clearly, in many countries, housing policies and implementation strategies, based on such project- or programme-level partnerships, call for substantial attitudinal and operational changes in municipal and national housing authorities (see Chapter 9).

7.1 The Case for Incremental Housing Strategies

The overall operational objectives of sustainable public sector engagement in the production of urban housing in partnership with the lowest income groups[3] are to:

- *stimulate the development* of formally recognised affordable housing, including rental housing, in approved locations and in sufficient quantities to address the needs of urban growth and make an impact on existing urban housing inadequacies (deficits);
- *build partnerships* between (local) government and private sector landowners and developers, where required to make affordable serviced land accessible to urban low-income group communities and households (see Section 8.1);
- *optimise public sector investment* in the provision of infrastructure and services to emerging, and existing, low-income neighbourhoods, including, where necessary, the development of partnerships with private sector and/or quango utility and service providers as well as with the beneficiary households and communities;
- *develop and support local organisational capacities* for the management of local development and community asset management and maintenance, including the nurture of sustained partnerships with NGOs (see Chapter 9).

Thus the six-point case for support to incremental housing production by the lowest urban income groups that is made in the sections that follow is on the understanding that to be effective and sustainable it must come through a 'package' that includes technical and financial assistance, income-generation opportunities, community and individual capacity building and community facilities, delivered through partnerships with government agencies, NGOs, private bodies and low-income communities themselves.

The 'Numbers' Case

The 'numbers' case for support to incremental housing largely rests on the fact that up to some 70 per cent of the urban population of developing cities already produce their housing incrementally, the majority of them informally (illegally) with little or no security of tenure, as described in Chapter 1. Furthermore, if government strategies are not put in place to recognise and support this process, it is projected that the world's urban slum population will grow from 830 million in 2010 to some two billion by the year 2050 (UN-Habitat 2003). The 'numbers case' is encapsulated in the dictum: 'If you can't beat them, join them' – *and in doing so, improve them*!

As recounted in Chapter 2, experience over the last 40 years of the twentieth century has clearly shown that neither countries nor cities have either the financial or the technical resources to produce affordable subsidised housing for more than a small fraction of their low-income urban populations in sufficient numbers, or at a rate, to match demand. Therefore, the most obvious strategy open to public housing agencies is to join, improve and formalise the informal processes that, as shown in Chapter 1, clearly work in terms of numbers and affordability, but tend to be imperfect in terms of security, health, safety and amenity – a resource that is generally ignored.

For instance, the 2015 National Shelter Strategy of Ghana stated that 'very little attempt has been made to harness and supplement people's own, non-conventional, strategies for procuring shelter for themselves and their families'. It went on to point out that the underlying problem that beset the country was that, although government had recognised the significance of non-conventional strategies for housing, it was confronted with a monstrous task of articulating such a complex issue into a refined process that could be promoted and implemented on a nationwide basis. The resulting lack of support for incremental housing was that approximately 90 per cent of the housing stock in Ghana was produced informally (CHF 2004).

Even in countries that have supported incremental housing through sites and services (S&S) projects and slum upgrading, the scale of the support has been so limited as to barely make a dent in housing needs. In Senegal, for example, a major programme of S&S projects, largely supported by the World Bank in the 1980s and 1990s had little impact on housing policy at the national level, which reverted to subsidising the building of finished homes by private sector developers and contractors for a small proportion of the middle- and upper-income groups, the consequence of which was that by 2007 illegal squatter settlements had grown to the extent that they housed more than 60 per cent of the population of metropolitan Dakar (Cohen 2007).

In summary, many governments still need to be convinced that investment in supporting local incremental housing production processes, initiated and implemented by urban low-income households and communities, provides a critical response to the urbanisation phenomenon that can lead to national economic growth and poverty reduction, and that 'conventional' housing policies, based on the formal (private) sector construction of subsidised dwellings that were being revived in the 1990s have virtually no impact on urban housing needs, leading to the proliferation of informal (illegal), invariably under-serviced, construction and urban development.

The Financial Case

The financial case for support to incremental housing is based on securing household investment in housing and community facilities. Secure housing is the greatest financial asset available to most urban families. The better the quality of a dwelling, the better its domestic facility, the greater is its exchange value, its value as collateral for borrowing and its price when it comes to selling. At the same time home ownership provides social security and status to its owners and occupants and the better the standard of the building and its immediate environment, generally the greater is its use value. Therefore, it is in the best interest of householders to invest in their housing, but only if their investment is secure. Few people will invest in property if there is any ambiguity in the legality of their title to it or in the physical safety of their asset. To a large extent it is the insecurity of title and/or location of informal settlements that create slums. Experience clearly shows that where security is ensured all but the very lowest of urban low-income groups, who have no surplus or savings at all, will invest time, energy and resources in extending and improving their dwelling and its surroundings. Thus, at relatively little or no cost to the state, good urban environments are created, enhancing public revenue in those towns and cities where local taxation is based on property values.

It has been estimated that small loans to low-income beneficiaries of the Sri Lanka Million Houses Programme (MHP) in the 1980s generated some of four to six times their value through the investment of family savings and informal borrowing, in addition to the value of labour and material inputs by the beneficiaries (see Section 4.1). The credit provided by the Dandora S&S project in Nairobi, Kenya, in the 1980s was augmented by a factor of four to five by individual household inputs (Lee-Smith & Memon 1988). In the Parcelles Assainies project in Dakar, the World Bank's Project Completion Report found that 'for every $1 of World Bank money provided, $8.20 of private funds were invested on site' (Rowbottom 1990). Thus by 2006, 'many houses in the project had two floors with six rooms on each, often with a third floor under construction, evidence of the willingness and capacity of households to invest in their homes' (Cohen 2007).

Security of tenure is not necessarily enough to generate the sort of multiplier on public sector financial inputs given in the above examples. The affordability of housing is determined by many financial issues that impinge upon householders' capacity to develop their dwellings. As pointed out in Chapter 2, in many early S&S schemes households were unable to afford the plots allocated to them in addition to increased transport, infrastructure and food costs, as well as find the resources needed to build a new house. However, other evidence suggests that with appropriately located plots, with affordable and easy access to services, plus even only minimal financial support packages for building, even very low-income households can mobilise considerable resources to build and improve their homes over time (see Case Studies 6–8, pp. 50–57).

The Urban Management Case

The urban management case for incremental housing strategies is premised on the principle of subsidiarity: the recognition of the most effective level or location of decision-making and authority for each component of an activity (see Section 3.2). Its application entails the identification of all public, private and community sector actors and their (potential) competences, and casting their roles accordingly.

With this understanding, the construction, maintenance and management of dwellings are logically the responsibility of households, not that of government. Only the owners and users of housing understand their own priorities for investment, their available resources and their changing needs in relation to their housing – and the level of risk that they are prepared to take. Government's role in the procurement of housing is that of facilitator, banker or guarantor, providing those inputs that households and communities cannot effectively or efficiently provide for themselves (e.g. the installation of off-site trunk infrastructure and service delivery). NGOs have often had key roles as intermediaries between low-income households and various departments of local and central government, as well as advisors and organisers. Different levels and departments of government have key, though not necessarily exclusive, roles in the supply and subdivision of land and the extension and management of infrastructure and urban services.

The process of supporting incremental housing strategies provides a unique vehicle for rationalising many urban management processes based on devolving or delegating many of governments' traditional responsibilities to the most appropriate (effective and efficient) actors, and developing partnerships with them (Riley & Wakely 2005).

A key role for government is the acquisition of suitably located land for low-income group housing, particularly where new sites are needed. Crucially, governments have the ability and authority to allocate public land for housing or to acquire it from private (illegal or legal) owners or to work in partnership with them in developing it for low-income group housing. Most significantly, governments themselves are often large-scale urban landowners. Public agencies and corporations such as railway, port and airport authorities and nationally owned industries that own large tracts of often vacant or underutilised urban land that is well serviced with urban infrastructure and good accessibility. Poor households can also have a potential role in finding and negotiating the transfer of land. For example, squatters in Mumbai, with NGO support, have mapped vacant land in the city and successfully negotiated its transfer in order that they may be resettled away from dangerous railway trackside slums (Patel & Mitlin 2004).

The management of the incremental extension and upgrading of infrastructure is not an easy process, particularly as, in addition to responding to the needs and demands of users, it is generally undertaken by different utility agencies or enterprises, as in the case of Rio de Janeiro's Favela Bairro programme, described in Section 4.2. However, as examples such as the Orangi Pilot Project in Karachi, Pakistan, have demonstrated, by coordinating organised community groups with different levels of government, effective and responsive systems can be developed that are not costly in either managerial or operational terms (Pervaiz et al. 2008).

In summary, state-supported incremental housing can act as a catalyst to the decentralisation of government in ways that improve the management of urban development and the administration of urban services, including the development of partnerships with private sector and community actors. Examples exist in which the private sector, both large companies and small and local enterprises, have been contracted for the installation and/or administration of infrastructure and the delivery of some services. In addition, public-private partnerships have been formed to legally develop and manage land for low-income incremental housing successfully (see: Section 8.1). NGOs have also worked with private enterprise to promote the effective use of infrastructure and support cost recovery procedures in informal settlements, as has been done in the Favela Bairro programme in Rio de Janeiro, Brazil, in partnerships between local NGOs and the private electricity company, Light (see Section 4.2 and Riley & Wakely 2005).

The Urban Development Case

Governments' engagement with incremental housing strategies provides an opportunity to regulate ongoing informal (illegal) urban development processes, and ensure adequate and relatively efficient provision for infrastructure and service delivery and the rational use of urban land. It therefore has the ability to shape the development of towns and cities in accordance with strategic priorities developed for an entire urban area, rather than just engaging in small-scale fire-fighting or the *post hoc* remedial upgrading of existing neighbourhoods.[4] Supported incremental housing can be a means to reduce uncontrolled low-density urban sprawl in favour of more efficient, high-density, compact development (Jenks & Burgess 2000).

In Dakar, Senegal, the absence of concerted, large-scale support for incremental housing in the 1980s resulted in low-density urban sprawl causing high infrastructure, energy and transport costs, environmental degradation problems and low levels of urban productivity and economic growth (Cohen 2007). By contrast, in Aleppo, Syria, before the 2010–2017 war that destroyed much of the city, informal settlements that housed 45 per cent of the urban population covered some 30 per cent of the developed area of the city, embracing both centrally located and peri-urban land. Whilst much of it served the occupants well in terms of location, it distorted land markets and presented a significant problem for the city's planners and those departments responsible for the administration of urban services. Formalising the informal settlements through the establishment of a municipal Informal Settlements Department in the Municipality of Aleppo (MoA) within the framework a city development strategy (CDS-Madinatuna) started to address these constraints to the city's development, with immediate results, such as the spontaneous establishment of local neighbourhood development committees that worked directly with the MoA Informal Settlements Department that linked them directly to the relevant infrastructure and services agencies (Wakely & Abdul-Wahab 2010).

The concern that even government supported self-build housing would be building 'official slums', particularly in city centre locations, has largely been refuted by the passage of time. Three decades after the first wave of S&S projects were implemented in cities in Asia, Africa and Latin America, many are indistinguishable from 'regular' neighbourhoods (Gattoni 2009). While 30 years may also see houses in unregulated squatter settlements reaching high-quality construction and environmental standards without any state assistance, many are characterised by disparities in housing standards, unsafe construction, illegal land tenure and precarious infrastructure and service levels. Officially supported incremental housing, by contrast, enables long-term infrastructure and service planning and the anticipation of future needs, and can provide the financial and technical assistance, as well as security, that can speed the local development of regular neighbourhoods within the context of planned urban growth. Incremental housing strategies can thus contribute not only to better urban development on a local scale but also to the development of cities as a whole, provided that they are planned as integrated components of the urban fabric, rather than isolated entities on the city fringes (Buckley et al. 2016; Fiori et al. 2014; Solana Oses 2013).

The Governance Case

The organisation and management of incremental building processes and particularly engagement in the installation and extension of neighbourhood infrastructure provides a means to the development of decentralised participatory decision-making and democratic governance. Good governance not only helps to ensure transparency and accountability in the management of the financial and physical aspects of housing and neighbourhood building, but it is also a vehicle for community development that can stimulate a wide range of productive local capacity building activities. Participation helps to create a sense of ownership and pride in the local environment that can engender a responsibility for the maintenance and management of community assets (streets, drains, street lighting, public open space, even schools and clinics). It reinforces the advantages and power of collaboration as opposed to competition for access to resources within urban low-income groups (Plummer 2002).

In the incremental process of house and neighbourhood building, in both slum upgrading programmes and S&S, projects have brought a mutual understanding between local leaders and government officials that hitherto had tended to be antagonistic. This was demonstrated, for instance, by the Busti Baseer Odhikar Surakha Committee (BOSC) structure, set up in Dhaka, Bangladesh in the late 1990s by the Coalition for the Urban Poor (CUP), an alliance of 53 NGOs, which established a citywide network of 'accountability mechanisms' to incorporate the urban poor in urban governance working with the city's ward commissioners, the lowest level of public administration. The BOSC structure was a hierarchy of elected committees, the base of which were primary committees representing some 500–1,000 households, which were then represented on (90) ward committees that in turn sent representatives to (29) *thana* committees and on to Dhaka City

Corporation. The ward commissioner, elected by his/her constituents, also provided the link to the city's service providers. This interface between government and organised representative non-governmental bodies became widely accepted and worked well in many of the city's wards, reportedly reducing corruption and giving voice and confidence (Banks 2008).

Slum/Shack Dwellers International (SDI) in Africa and India and the Asian Coalition for Housing Rights (ACHR) are international federations of NGO-supported slum dwellers with a strong message of developing mutual understanding between urban low-income communities and government by working on the premise of nurturing mutual appreciation of the aims, ambitions, strengths and constraints faced by both local officials and low-income communities (D'Cruz & Satterthwaite 2005). In the best of circumstances such appreciation leads to mutual understanding and the development of trust and eventually to active 'city building' partnerships. These are the foundations of progressive urban governance that can grow out of direct engagement in the implementation of incremental housing policies and practices (Riley & Wakely 2005).

The Social and Economic Development Case

Closely allied to fostering good governance, incremental housing processes can be an important and effective catalyst to the social and economic development of poor households and communities. As pointed out above, organising themselves (or being organised) to engage in developing their housing and local environment inevitably brings people together in a 'common cause'. In the past, this has been especially dramatic and important in those S&S projects in which the beneficiaries were randomly selected (i.e. not a 'by-product' of slum relocation in which existing communities are moved as a whole). This has presented an opportunity to develop and consolidate social solidarity and to introduce and support local enterprise initiatives and employment, notably in the infrastructure and house construction activities of settlement upgrading or in S&S projects themselves. But they have also built social capital around issues that were not directly related to the immediate urban environment, developing wider networks and involving other groups, for example sporting or cultural activities that engaged the youth, and NGO programmes for anything ranging from women's literacy to environmental health, nutrition and home economics.

A range of successful examples of such strategies exist. For instance, central to the Dandora S&S project in Nairobi, Kenya, in the 1980s was the establishment of a Community Development Division of the Project Department that managed the organisation of house builder groups and made links to other, citywide welfare organisations and social programmes

(Lee-Smith & Memon 1988). Specially trained community workers played a similar 'citizen-building' role in both the S&S and upgrading components of the Lusaka housing projects of the mid-1970s (Jere 1984) and likewise in Indonesia's extensive Kampong Improvement Programme in Jakarta, Surabaya and Bandung (Silas 1984).

The strategic importance of locally managed savings groups as a vehicle for community building and nurturing solidarity, particularly among women engaged in incremental house building, has become well understood. Not only can the regular daily or weekly saving of very small amounts of money generate significant capital funds for borrowing but the process of collecting, banking, lending and recovering loans is also a powerful means of community building and the development of grassroots collective management capacities. Such savings schemes underpin the activities of the National Slum Dwellers Federation and Mahila Milan in India and their partners in Shack/Slum Dwellers International (Mitlin 2008). In Cambodia, the Urban Poor Development Fund has supported a large number of community-based savings groups in Phnom Penh and provided loans and grants for land acquisition as well as for upgrading, house building, income generation enterprises and food production, and developed better relations with government (Phonphakdee et al. 2009). The success and impact of the Sri Lanka Women's Bank, which started as a small housing-related savings-and-loans scheme in Colombo in the early 1990s and had locally controlled and managed branches in 22 of the country's 25 administrative districts by the year 2000, is described at length in Section 4.1.

Both the location and the provision of facilities for income-generating activities in incremental housing projects have had an important impact on poverty reduction and householders' capacity to improve their housing. As an example, workshop facilities were planned into the Shivaji Park S&S project in Alwar, India, that, together with the project's central location, had an important impact on women's participation in work. Many women started new enterprises, mainly tailoring and other clothing-related activities, working from home and supplying local formal sector retailers. Follow-up surveys showed that this increased the number of working family members from less than one to an average of 2.5 and household incomes by six to eight times, between 1985 and 2000 (Lall 2002).

In conclusion, the process of supporting the incremental process of building and improving housing and neighbourhoods can provide the basis for the wider social and economic development of low-income households and communities. However, it also means that many government and municipal departments responsible for housing and works have to take on or develop their capacity to provide social and economic supports, requiring new sets of skills and professional competencies that many housing authorities have not traditionally had. For instance, the 1970s Dandora S&S project in Nairobi, mentioned above, led the City Council to establish a new permanent Housing Development Department with a strong Community Development Division. The Sri Lanka National Housing Development Authority had to retrain its cadre of building technicians to enable them to take on new roles as community support advisors in order to implement the national Million Houses Programme in the early 1980s (see Section 4.1).

7.2 Rental Housing

As pointed out at the end of Section 3.2, for a large proportion of low-income urban households, the freehold ownership of urban property is low amongst their livelihood priorities. Indeed, for many, especially the very poor and recent or itinerant migrants to the city, it cannot be entertained at all because they have neither the financial nor the social resources, or inclination to invest in and maintain urban real estate (Lonardoni & Bolay 2016). However, it has been demonstrated that all but the totally destitute are able and willing to pay a recurrent rent for accommodation, provided it ensures an acceptable level of physical, financial and legal security over a sustained period of time.[5]

Therefore, any urban housing policy and strategy for its implementation must embrace an adequate supply of affordable rental accommodation, which, when left to the private sector, has frequently been corrupt and exploitative. In response governments have attempted to address rent exploitation and extortion with control legislation that inevitably is difficult to administer and open to abuse, as well as tending to have a negative impact on the housing market and the quality and maintenance of the rental housing stock. Landlords are reluctant to deplete their profits by investing in remedial maintenance of their rented-out property.

The limitations and failures of statutory rent control legislation, referred to in Chapter 3, mean that, in many cities new approaches need to be found to securing legal title to rental accommodation and assuring its affordability to low-income group tenants, while remaining financially attractive to formal and informal private sector landlords. An obvious and well-tried approach has been the construction, maintenance and management of rental housing by government housing agencies ('conventional' public housing, as described in Section 2.1), that was abandoned in most countries largely because housing agencies were unable to sustain the 'landlord costs' of its maintenance and management.

Nevertheless, there is a good argument for a return to 'conventional' public rental housing, in which (local/municipal) governments retain responsibility for the production of housing units and financial control of affordable (subsidised) rents, whilst the day-to-day administration and maintenance of buildings and infrastructure, including rent and service charge collection, is managed by local democratically constituted CBOs representing the beneficiary tenants. Hitherto, such public-private partnerships have rarely been adopted in developing cities, though they have been approximated, for example by formally constituted and regulated housing associations in the United Kingdom.[6] In many cities, there is likely to be a conflict in the location and design of such public/community rental housing, between high-density multi-storey development in convenient city-centre locations, where land values are high, and lower density housing on or beyond the urban periphery where undeveloped land is relatively cheaper. Such conflicts can only be resolved by negotiation between housing authorities and the leadership of potential beneficiary communities who understand the particularities of domestic and communal space use.

Such a strategy depends upon close partnership relationships between the public agencies, playing the capitalist-developer role and occupant CBOs that play the subordinate management role of administrating the housing in use, having also been an 'authentic' partner in the primary location and design decisions,[7] and should not be confused with the least successful aspects of the 'conventional' public housing strategies of the 1960s and 1970s, described in Section 2.1, in which the tenants of public housing had no real responsibility for their housing, other than paying the rent, and were rarely even consulted about their housing and related needs and demands in use, let alone in the early location, planning and design stages of production.

The private sector provision of socially acceptable rental accommodation that is affordable to low-income households is commonplace in most informal settlements in developing cities, filling a need for the accommodation of rent-paying low-income group tenants and providing or augmenting the incomes of equally low-income landlords (Kumar 1996).[8] Generally this process works well; it provides affordable housing, though of course it is not always perfect and equitable; corruption and exploitation of both tenants and, less frequently, landlords exists, though by-and-large, the system of low-income (informal) renting meets the needs of tenants and supplements the grassroots economy (Kumar 2001). However, in many situations, there is a need for government support to extend and improve it, though to attempt to regulate it would be likely to endanger its market effectiveness. Because of (informal) market imperfections, it is not always numerically adequate, leaving some families with no alternative to absolute homelessness or the most precarious forms of squatting (e.g. on pavements, road and railway verges, etc.).

A range of different approaches to stimulating the provision of private rental housing exist, most of them in developed countries of the Global North and based on cash grants and tax concessions that are only attractive to formal sector tax payers. In developing cities, financial incentives in the form of cash grants and/or immunity from legal sanctions have been given for the construction or extension of existing dwellings for rent, most often as part of informal settlement upgrading programmes or projects, such as the Plan Terrazas Programme in Colombia in the 1970s, successfully implemented in the cities of Bogotá, Medellin and Cali (UN-Habitat 2005).

Another interesting example, also from the 1970s, was a proposal for Chandigarh, the new capital of the Indian states of Punjab and Haryana. The two state government administrations and that of the Chandigarh Union Territory (city) generated a very large proportion of the city's total employment in public sector jobs. Government departments and agencies were statutorily required to contribute to the housing of their employees, which meant that a significant amount of public – state and city administration – expenditure was devoted to 'housing allowances' that subsidised the payment of private sector rents by low-income employees (junior clerical and manual workers). To reduce this expenditure as well as contribute to the city's low-income group housing stock, it was proposed that part of the government housing allowance budget should be used to provide 'soft' loans to low-income employees to build, or extend their houses in such a way that they could accommodate a tenant household as well as their own family. Under this arrangement, it was to be agreed that the extra accommodation (in effect, a second dwelling) would be let to the government Housing Department at an agreed fixed rate for a fixed period (eight years). The government would then on-let it to another low-income employee, applying a subsidy, if required. At the end of the fixed term, which was to coincide with the closure of the amortisation period of the initial loan, the rented dwelling would revert to the landlord/owner who built it, to occupy or rent out again on the open market, thereby continuing, and probably increasing, his/her supplementary income.

This model of minimal public sector support to the production of affordable low-income group rental housing, in this case in the peculiar conditions of the new town of Chandigarh in the 1970s, a large, fast-growing administrative centre, could be applied in a modified form by any municipal or metropolitan housing authority.

In conclusion, adaptable examples and precedents exist for potentially economic, efficient, equitable and flexible approaches to the provision of support to the development of affordable rental housing for urban low-income groups through different types of partnerships between local (municipal or metropolitan) government and private (informal) sector landlords and housing entrepreneurs, as well as public rental housing, constructed by government housing authorities in partnership with its beneficiary households and community organisations.

Notes

1 Incremental procurement of urban housing is not confined to low-income house-holds. Almost all permanent and serviced housing is procured as an incremental process that takes place over relatively long periods of time. Upper- and middle-income group households with regular incomes and collateral guarantees have access to long-term credit – housing loans and mortgages – that may take between 15 and 30 years of incremental repayments to redeem.
2 See: https://en.wikipedia.org/wiki/partnership
3 As prescribed by the UN's New Urban Agenda (2016) and the Sustainable Development Goals (2015), most pertinently SDG11.
4 Studies in Bogotá, Colombia, in the 1990s showed that the cost of developing serviced land for low-income group housing was almost one third of the cost regularising established informal settlements (Fernandes 2011).
5 In the early 1970s, on the basis of his experience in informal *barriadas* in Lima, Peru, John F.C. Turner developed a simple but robust model of the progress of low-income earners' changing needs and priorities for housing and other livelihood assets as they progress through different income groups and degrees of adaptation to, and integration in, urban society and economy (Turner 1972), that has stood the tests of time and much subsequent urban social-anthropological research.
6 See www.Wikipedia.org/wiki/Housing_Association.
7 See: Riley & Wakely (2005) *Communities and Communication: Building Urban Partnerships*, pp. 11–29, for a discussion on 'authentic partnerships . . . founded on trust, mutualism, interdependency, legitimacy and respect' in the sharing of both risks and benefits of investing resources and energy in housing and local development.
8 Sunil Kumar (1996) identifies three categories of urban informal landlords in India: (1) subsistence landlords, who often are poorer than the tenants to whom they rent out rooms in order to supplement their family incomes; (2) petty commodity landlords, for whom their income from renting accommodation repre-sents an essential component of their household incomes; and (3) petty capitalist landlords, who may own several properties as a primary source of income, which in some developing cities can be quite substantial.

References

Banks, N., 2008, 'A tale of two wards: Political participation and the urban poor in Dhaka city', *Environment & Urbanization*, Vol. 20, No. 2, Sage, London, UK.
Buckley, R.M., A. Kallergis & L. Wainer, 2016, 'Addressing the housing challenge: Avoiding the Ozmandias Syndrome', *Environment & Urbanization*, Vol. 28, No. 1, London, UK.
CHF, 2004, Strategic Assessment of the Affordable Housing Sector in Ghana, CHF International, Silver Spring, MD, USA.
Cohen, M., 2007, 'Aid, density and urban form: Anticipating Dakar', *Built Environment*, Vol. 33, No. 2, Alexandrine Press, Oxford, UK.
D'Cruz, C. & D. Satterthwaite, 2005, Building Homes, Changing Official Approaches: The Work of Urban Poor Organisations and their Federations and their Contributions to meeting the Millennium Development Goals, IIED Poverty reduction in urban areas working paper 16, London, UK.

Fernandes, E., 2011, Regularization of Informal Settlements in Latin America, Policy Focus Report Series, Lincoln Institute of Land Policy, Cambridge MA, USA.

Fiori, J., H. Hinsley & L.

Barth (eds), 2014, *Housing as Urbanism: Critical Reflections on the Brazilian Experience of Urban Housing*, Architectural Association, London, UK.

Gattoni, G., 2009, 'A case for the incremental housing in sites-and-services programs', paper presented at IDB conference, July, http://idbdocs.iadb.org/ WSDocs/getDocument.aspx?DOCNUM-2062811 (accessed, Nov.2016)

Jenks, M. & R. Burgess (eds), 2000, Compact Cities. Sustainable Urban Forms for Developing Countries, Spon Press, London, UK.

Jere, H., 1984, 'Lusaka: Local participation in planning and decision-making' in Payne, G.K. (ed.) *Low Income Housing in the Developing World: The Role of Sites and Services and Settlement Upgrading*, Wiley, Chichester, UK.

Kumar, S., 2001, *Social Relations, Rental Housing Markets & the Poor in Urban India*, Department of Social Policy, London School of Economics and Political Science, London, UK.

Kumar, S., 1996, 'Subsistence and petty-capitalist landlords: A theoretical framework for the analysis of landlordism in Third World low-income settlements', *International Journal of Urban and Regional Research*, Vol. 20 No. 2, Wiley, London, UK.

Lee-Smith, D. & Memon, P., 1988, 'Institution development for delivery of low-income housing: An evaluation of Dandora Community Development Project in Nairobi', *Third World Planning Review*, Vol. 10 No. 3, Liverpool, UK.

Lonardoni, F. & J.C. Bolay, 2016, 'Rental housing and the urban poor: Understanding the growth and production of Rental housing in Brazilian *favelas*', *International Journal of Urban Sustainable Development*, Vol. 8 No. 1, Taylor & Francis, Abingdon, UK.

Mitlin, D., 2008, *Urban Poor Funds: Development by the People for the People*, IIED Poverty Reduction in Urban Areas Working Paper 18, IIED, London UK.

Patel, S. & D. Mitlin, 2004, 'The work of SPARC, The National Slum Dwellers Federation and Mahila Milan', in Mitlin, D. & D. Satterthwaite (eds) *Empowering Squatter Citizens: The Roles of Local Governments and Civil Society in Reducing Urban Poverty*, Earthscan, London, UK.

Pervaiz, A., P. Rahman & A. Hasan, 2008, Lessons from Karachi: The role of Demonstration, Documentation, Mapping and Relationship Building in Advocacy for Improved Urban Sanitation and Water Services, IIED Human Settlements Discussion Paper: Water-6, London,

Phonphakdee, S., Visal, S. & Sauter, G., 2009, '*The Urban Poor Development Fund in Cambodia: supporting local and citywide development*', *Environment & Urbanization*, Vol. 21, No. 2, Sage, London, UK.

Plummer, J., 2002, *Focusing Partnerships: A Sourcebook for Municipal Capacity Building in Public-Private Partnerships*, Earthscan, London, UK.

Riley, E. & P. Wakely, 2005, *Communities and Communication: Building Urban Partnerships*, ITDG Publishing, Rugby, UK.

Rowbottom, S., 1990, *Senegal Case Study, Parcelles Assaines: From Project to Place – After Three Decades*, CHF Occasional Paper, Vol.3, CHF International, Silver Spring, MD, USA.

Silas, J., 1984, 'The Kampong Improvement Programme of Indonesia: A comparative case study of Jakarta and Surabaya', in Payne, G.K. (ed.) *Low Income Housing in the Developing World*, Wiley, Chichester, UK.

Solana Oses, O. 2013, *Affordable Housing and Urban Sprawl in Mexico: The Need for a Paradigm Shift*, University of Manchester, Global Urban Research Centre, Briefing Paper No. 4, Manchester, UK.

Turner, J.F.C., 1972, 'Housing as a verb, in Turner, J.F.C. & R. Fichter (eds), *Freedom to Build: Dweller Control of the Housing Process*, Macmillan, New York, USA.

UN-Habitat, 2003, *The Challenge of Slums: Global Report on Human Settlements 2003*, (revised 2010), Earthscan, London, UK.

UN-Habitat, 2005, Financing Urban Shelter: Global Report on Human Settlements 2005, Earthscan, London, UK.

Wakely, P. & R. Abdul-Wahab, 2010, *Informal Land and Housing Markets in Aleppo, Syria*, [English and Arabic], GIZ, Eschborn, Germany.

8 Components of Support to Incremental Development

Having established that the latest paradigm shift has been from participation and 'enabling' to 'partnership', this chapter focuses on the components of support that need to be provided for the implementation of urban incremental housing programmes and projects, in which householders and community leaders, in partnership with local government and other key stakeholders, take responsibility for the development of their dwellings and neighbourhood infrastructure and services, employing their own (small) contractors and suppliers. Emphasis is inevitably given to processes for the production of the 'hardware' of housing (buildings and infrastructure works), though attention must simultaneously be given to the provision of social and cultural development as well as enhancing management and local governance skills at the community/neighbourhood level.

8.1 Land and Location

Land is perhaps the principal component of government support to housing for urban low-income groups. Government influences the availability of land through:

- allocating and using publicly owned land;
- expanding infrastructure and services to new sites, enabling their development;
- administering rules and regulations such as planning laws, building permits and development controls that impact on its price and availability; and through
- the efficiency and transparency with which these are applied (E&U 2009).

In making land available for incremental development consideration needs to be given to three basic aspects: its location, price and the title conditions under which it is transferred to its occupants and users.

Cost and Location

The selection of land for the incremental development of low-income hous-ing is difficult though crucial to the success of any incremental housing policy or project. Peri-urban land has often been acquired because of its relatively low price, only to find that the cost of extending infrastructure to it renders it unaffordable to the target groups. With no provision for afford-able transport links to employment centres, commerce and community facilities, poor location was one of the keys to the unpopularity and failure of many sites and services (S&S) schemes in the 1980s and accounted for the preponderance of empty plots and the rapid turnover of residents (Van der Linden 1992).

There are many anecdotal accounts from the past that illustrate the impor-tance of location to low-income families living on minimal and precarious incomes: for instance, of a squatter tenant in an illegal and insecure shanty in Mexico City making a basic living from casual employment as a semi-skilled mason on city centre building sites who with his wife, who ran a kiosk serving tourists, was awarded secure title to an 'affordable', well-serviced, though basic, house on the urban periphery, thereby increasing his transport and housing costs from 5 per cent of his monthly expenditure to 55 per cent, forcing him and his family to abandon their new dwelling and seek alterna-tive rental accommodation in another centrally located informal settlement (Turner 1976). Such stories of households abandoning serviced sites and subsidised housing with secure title on the urban fringes and returning to the precarious existence of squatting in shacks with no infrastructure, but located close job opportunities and community ties, come from around the world.[1]

In Guyana, one of the failings of the Inter-American Development Bank (IDB)-supported Low Income Settlements Programme (LISP) in the 1990s was the location of land:

> distant from existing infrastructure and services leading to low occu-pancy rates due to affordability issues (people could not afford to build houses) and infrastructure and service deficiencies. Sites were on agricultural land in distant locations where transport costs were too high. Because of the high cost of extending trunk infrastructure to the site, support services such as schools, clinics and playing fields were planned for but not built. There was no commerce on site and no nearby employment.
>
> (Gattoni 2009)

Food also tends to be more expensive in peripheral locations and adds to overall increases in expenditure (Cohen 2007). Similarly in El Salvador,

FUSAU-Integral, a company that promoted integrated housing solutions, found that the main constraints to scaling up its work were the lack of suitable and affordable land, high costs of the provision of basic services and the distance of available land from sources of employment.

In the past, the planners of S&S projects have often ignored the social impact of settling thousands of people far from urban centres, failing to support the building of new community networks, social cohesion or local management capacities. Relocation involves the loss of socio-spatial support networks, a loss that the poor are least able to afford, and it takes time to build new networks (Van der Linden 1992). New settlements near existing centres of commerce, employment and housing have almost invariably done better, for example, many of those moving to Khuda-ki-Basti near Hyderabad in Pakistan had relatives nearby, suggesting that this, the location of the project, was an important aspect of their decision to resettle in the project (see Case Study 4, p. 42).

Thus, evidence from successful projects suggests that new incremental housing projects that aim to generate stable and vibrant communities are those that are within the city limits and near to existing employment, services and infrastructure, despite cost constraints and concerns for the relatively short-term 'unsightliness' of low-income settlements in process of phased construction by stages.

The successful 1980s Shivaji Park S&S project in Alwar, India, was located just 3 km from major office complexes where all major services and social and physical infrastructure were easily accessible, schools were within 4–6 km from the new settlement, and a main hospital was within 2 km. Also, retail and wholesale markets were nearby and high- and medium-income public and private housing complexes surrounded the settlement. Those working in micro-enterprises stimulated by the project travelled less than 1 km to work. Those working as home-based manufacturers travelled no more than 3 km to fetch materials from central neighbourhoods and deliver products to retailers, while the maximum workplace commute was 6 km, travelled by about one-third of the employed residents. Thus the project stimulated local economic development by virtue of fostering workplaces within the settlement itself but also owing to its advantageous location near the town centre. The central location of Shivaji Park also enabled greater access to education facilities, resulting in a student drop out rate in the seven- to ten-year-old age range much lower than in other resettled low-income communities located on the edge of the town (Lall 2002).

S&S projects within urban areas in the 1990s usually entailed developing relatively small parcels of land, unlike the vast projects of the 1970s and 1980s on the urban fringes, such as the enormous Arumbakkam project on the Western fringes of Madras (Chennai), India, with 2,300 plots, that benefited from both the relatively low capital cost of land and from economies of scale. However, it has been found that the higher costs of working at a small scale on more central sites are offset by relatively easy connection to existing trunk infrastructure and access to existing services. While individual land parcels (infill sites) may be small, the number of suitable sites within cities is usually large, enabling over-all programme scales to be significant, as demonstrated by the Favela Bairro programme in Rio de Janeiro, Brazil, described in Section 4.2.

In summary, the identification of land on which to develop incremental low-income housing projects requires a much more rigorous analysis of its costs and benefits than merely its initial price and the cost of servicing it. It also entails an assessment of the social and economic costs in use by the intended beneficiaries in a context of often wildly fluctuating family for-tunes, insecure incomes and changing household priorities. Attempts may be made to model such variables, but it is unlikely that any such exercise would have much use in practice. However, more down-to-earth methods do exist and have proved highly successful. For instance, with the assis-tance of the non-governmental organisation (NGO) coalition between the National Slum Dwellers Federation of India (NSDF), Mahila Milan and the Society for the Promotion of Area Resource Centres (SPARC),[2] organised groups of pavement dwellers in Mumbai, India, have themselves identified vacant land that would meet their requirements in terms of location and negotiated with government for its acquisition and terms for its develop-ment and transfer to them for their occupation (Patel & Mitlin 2004). A similar approach has been adopted in Phnom Penh, Cambodia, with the support of the NGO Asian Coalition for Housing Rights (ACHR), where squatter households not only sought appropriate land within the city that government could acquire, but also, with the volunteering assistance of young urban planners and architects of the Phnom Penh Urban Resource Centre (URC), presented the housing authority with proposals for its sub-division into plots and a financial development plan that would meet their needs and resource constraints (ACHR 2004).

These examples involve the relocation of existing urban communities. In 'open application' programmes and projects the identification of sites can only be undertaken by the development agency, or in partnership with landowners and/or developers. The take-up of sites then is dependent upon their 'marketability', which embraces all the criteria and priorities of the potential takers, and the beneficiary selection process (see Section 8.4).

Land Acquisition and Law Reform

Well-located privately owned land within an existing built-up area is invari-ably likely to command high prices, normally well beyond the capacity of local government social housing budgets, necessitating recourse to compulsory purchase by government.

Compulsory acquisition is the power of government to acquire private rights in land without the willing consent of its owner or occupant in order to benefit society. This power is often necessary for social and economic development and the protection of the natural environment. Compulsory acquisition requires finding the balance between the public need for land on the one hand, and the provision of land tenure security and the protection of private property rights on the other hand. Compulsory acquisition is inherently disruptive. Even when compensation is generous and procedures are generally fair and efficient, the displacement of people from established homes, businesses and communities still entails significant human costs. Where the process is not designed or implemented well, the economic, social and political costs may be enormous. Attention to the procedures of compulsory acquisition is critical if a government's exercise of compulsory acquisition is to be efficient, fair and legitimate (McAuslan 1985).

Compulsory acquisition of land for low-income housing, where such legal power exists, requires considerable political will and risk that few politicians will entertain. So governments have to negotiate with private landowners using incentives to encourage them to make land available, or to develop it themselves, on terms that are affordable to low-income householders – usually below the optimum market returns. For instance, in the 1990s the Maharashtra Slum Rehabilitation Authority in India administered an incentive scheme of transferable development rights (TDR) through which private sector landowners and developers could obtain attractive advantages for the profitable development of commercially marketable land in exchange for the release of appropriately located land for low-income housing development at sub-prime rates. The Malaysian government Public Low-Cost Housing Program (PLHP) 1996–2000 required private sector developers to make a minimum of 30 per cent of land or houses available at sub-market prices affordable to low-income households as a condition for the issue of development permits for profitable commercial housing for middle- and upper-income groups (Bakhtyar et al. 2013).

At a local level, there have been strategies such as 'land-sharing', whereby government negotiates with the owners of urban land that has been (illegally) settled by squatters, thereby rendering it worthless in formal market terms, for the transfer of a portion of their land, in exchange for the other portion of their land to be legally cleared of squatters by the relevant public sector authorities, which the owner could then use profitably or develop commercially. The other part of land is returned to its (squatter) occupants with legally recognised secure title, to be upgraded/redeveloped by them, usually at higher residential densities, as the negotiated land usually has to accommodate at least some of the occupants of the cleared portion of the land that was returned to the landlord. Such land-sharing strategies were highly successful in Bangkok, Thailand, in the early 1980s (Angel & Chirathamkijkul 1983) and have also been employed in Chennai, India, amongst other places.

The lack of planning and budgeting for future low-income group settlements remains a persistent problem for urban planning and housing authorities. However, working with community organisations to develop land cadastres can provide powerful information to help push an agenda for land market reforms that are usually complicated and often inequitable. Not only can poor households and community leaders drive incremental house construction and improvement, but they can be active agents in getting land for housing, either through negotiating tenure for the land they occupy or negotiating new sites on which they can build, as illustrated by the NSDF in India, described above (Patel & Mitlin 2004). Federations of community organisations and NGOs can make cadastres of land, conduct surveys and cost the work that needs to be done to develop new sites. In Bangladesh, it has been argued that NGOs should take a more active part in low-income group incremental housing schemes, help negotiate land transfers, advocate that land titles be decoupled from service provision, promote techniques such as plot reconstitution and guided land development, verify land records, supervise procurement and validate transactions (Rahman 2005).

The nature and scale of the challenges of national land law reform, especially in urban areas that have grown in a spontaneous and chaotic fashion, are complex and volatile, but they are becoming better understood by such programmes as the UN-Habitat Global Land Tool Network[3] that is able to demonstrate workable strategies and bring pressure to bear on governments for the introduction of reforms in this politically sensitive and socially volatile area.

Many cities have extensive 'reserves' of under-utilised urban land in public ownership, usually by such agencies as port or railway authorities and the military that no longer require central urban locations that could be transferred to low-income group housing. However, such are the complexities of inter-agency relations that negotiating such transfers has rarely been easy. The re-designation and redevelopment of vast areas of obsolete privately owned industrial land and Port Authority-owned land, suitable for low-income group housing and public open space, in central Mumbai, India, is a dramatic example (d'Monte 2006)

Strategies such as city land banking can be developed on a long-term perspective, in which central or municipal government acquires low priced peri-urban agricultural or waste land for development in the future when its commercial value is likely to have risen as a result of urban expansion.

The often-quoted example of this type of long-term strategy is the city of Stockholm, Sweden, which acquired extensive rural land for unspecified future development, at the beginning of the twentieth century. But there are others. For instance, in the early 1970s Syria conducted a national programme of compulsory peri-urban land acquisition that left municipalities with extensive reserves of state owned suburban land. By default, it also brought large areas of land onto the informal market at prices affordable to the lowest income groups, which were still higher than the official compensation prices paid by the government. Thus in 1972, peri-urban landowners scrambled to sell their property informally to the highest (low-income) bidder before official compulsory acquisition orders could be issued. Another successful example is that of the Iran Urban Land Act 1979 that created 'banks' of publically owned land, affordable to urban low-income groups that operated alongside the private sector land markets (Keivani et al. 2008).

Tenure and Title

In many societies individual freehold ownership of land and property is the only form of title considered absolutely secure by low-income households who are making or consolidating their positions and lifestyles in the city. However, it is not the only option open to low-income group incremental housing and it has been criticised in the past for enabling households to sell their plots up-market, for example in S&S projects, thereby speculating with, and making profits from, government subsidies. Various forms of collective title such as housing associations, cooperatives and condominiums can provide acceptable mechanisms to limit such speculation. These, and other forms of community land trusts (CLTs) need not prevent individual householders from transferring their property but they can guard against speculation with it before its full cost, or market value, has been redeemed. Such alternative forms of tenure and collective management can provide low-income groups with protection from market forces and support the building of community, as well as improve affordability (Payne et al. 2009).

Long and renewable leasehold titles to land are not out of the question for incremental housing, though they are rarely socially acceptable. As described in Section 4.1, the Sri Lanka Million Houses Programme (MHP) in the 1980s issued plots on 15-year leases, as it was argued that urban land should remain in public ownership in order to facilitate unforeseeable future changes in use. Initially there was no indication that this deterred households from investing in the construction, extension and improvement of their houses, or contributing to the upgrading or installation of neighbourhood infrastructure or service facilities. However, under pressure from leaseholders, the tenure periods were extended to 30, then 50 years, until finally all were transferred to full freehold title in 2008 (Wakely 2008).

In conclusion, all the evidence shows that a sustainable supply of well-located, affordable land is essential to successful state-supported incremental housing initiatives. Innovative tools and techniques to acquire land are available (Angel & Chirathamkijkul 1983) and plot sizes and housing densities can be manipulated to bring down per capita costs of land. However, a political will to reform urban land markets that can be sustained over time and across changes in political regime, is fundamental to ensuring the supply of land for low-income housing. Community organisations and NGOs can play a significant role in building and sustaining that political will (E&U 2009; McAuslan 1985).

In the first decades of the twenty-first century there was an increasingly active move to promote the commons 'ownership' of urban land, such as CLTs, delinking it, in valuation terms, from the property or any other development on or in it (Lewis & Conaty 2012).

8.2 Finance[4]

In early S&S and slum upgrading projects the provision of finance to enable the house construction process was not generally considered to be government responsibility. Yet one of the perceived failures of many such projects was the slow progress of construction, most often because households did not have the resources to build in addition to paying their contributions to the cost of land and infrastructure. However, as pointed out in Chapter 3, in other projects the opposite was often true – even very low-income households have been able to raise considerable amounts of funding independently. Access to credit as part of a support package needs to be considered with caution and preferably in terms of small short-term loans.

The credit needs of incremental housing differs significantly from conventional housing (mortgage) finance, which is based on funding the procurement of ready-built dwellings or to build complete houses as a once-only event. Credit for the incremental construction of housing by low-income families is very different. Large long-term loans, committing households to sustained debt burdens, are almost exactly what low-income families, who are making their way in the urban economy and society, do not need or want. What are required for incremental house construction are flexible, relatively small, short-term loans that are responsive to the intermittent demands of households' changing fortunes and priorities. Many years may elapse between different stages of house building; small loans may be needed to waterproof a roof or larger loans to build a second storey, and so on. Such finance facilities are rarely available in the conventional supply-led housing finance and mortgage markets. The closest approximations tend to be schemes that provide demand-led small scale credit for enterprise development, generally assessed on the risk rating of the proposed business returns and not on the collateral provided by a borrower's property.

There are financing (security) advantages in making even initial starter loans for construction available on an incremental basis requiring borrowers to 'qualify' for the next stage of credit only by completing the previous stage(s). For example the Sri Lanka MHP issued credit for construction of new houses in three basic instalments: the first instalment for the foundations and floor slab; second, the structure to eaves level; and a third/final instalment for the cost of the roof, all of which would cover the total construction cost of a basic dwelling. The cost of any additions, such as internal walls and finishes, had to be found by the house builder (GoSL 1983). This worked well, though checking and approving the completion of work on each stage and authorising successive instalments put a heavy administrative burden on the already overstretched government housing officers in the early stages of the programme, so this responsibility was subsequently devolved to local community-based organisations (CBOs) (the Community Development Councils – see Section 4.1).

In order to ensure that financial support is invested in incremental house construction as intended by cautious housing authorities and (paternalistic) aid donors, an alternative to monetary credit has been the provision of building materials, bought in bulk by housing authorities and passed on to authorised house builders at or below cost. However, it was often found that such schemes were open to exploitation. For instance, in the Camplands S&S project in Kingston, Jamaica, in the 1970s, many householders sold their project-allocated cement, steel, timber and roofing sheets on the open market for a profit and constructed their dwellings with new or second-hand materials that they could acquire even cheaper in the informal market. In other instances this has not been a problem and on-site organised depots of building materials, bought and stored in bulk, have proved able to lower the cost of construction materials and served as 'one-stop-shops' for building materials, technical and managerial advice and housing loan disbursements, though they have been known to drive out local small-scale suppliers who were a source of local employment and incomes.

In more recent programmes in several countries, independent credit facilities and management have been shown to be more efficient and effective than those administered by government. For example, the micro credit programmes supported by the Swedish International Development Cooperation Agency (SIDA) and managed by NGOs in Central America, in the late 1980s, provided credit specifically tailored to local housing and infrastructure needs, with its administration coordinated with the provision of technical advice to house builders along the lines described above (Stein & Vance 2008). While NGOs in Bangladesh provided little credit targeted specifically at housing, it was frequently found that the loans that they administered for income generation projects were actually used to fund housing improvements (Rahman 2005). The plethora of microfinance initiatives for enterprise development, both small and large in scale and either community-managed or supported by NGOs (or banks), attests to the ability of poor people to mobilise resources and apply long-term financial strategies at low risk, or no risk, to lenders. However, this form of microfinance has rarely embraced credit specifically for the construction, extension and improvement of housing that does not necessarily directly produce monetary returns.

8.3 Infrastructure and Services

The timing, standard and level of infrastructure and service[5] provision is a key component of support to incremental housing initiatives. In the past, where S&S projects have provided infrastructure and services at the outset of the project at too high a level, costs have proved unaffordable for low-income households and higher income groups have bought them out. Where infrastructure and service standards have been too low (below expectations), or their installation delayed, house building has remained undeveloped and projects unattractive to all income groups. So a careful balance has to be struck. This is best done by returning to the principle of subsidiarity. In theory decisions concerning the level of infrastructure provision can only equitably and effectively be made at the level of the community of users, distinguishing between the different needs of men and women, girls and boys, provided that all decision-makers fully understand the implications of the trade-offs between initial capital cost, cost in use and the inherent tenets of environmental health, safety and amenity provided by good quality infrastructure and services, including the future risks occasioned by climate change and other natural hazards, such as flooding and earthquakes (UN-Habitat 2011).

Community action planning (CAP), pioneered in Sri Lanka in the 1980s (see Section 4.1), is one of a series of techniques to engage low-income communities in establishing priorities and setting standards for infrastructure and service provision based on a thorough understanding of the costs and benefits of their decisions (Hamdi & Goethert 1997). However, this may not always be practicable, for instance in situations where new communities are being formed. In the S&S resettlement component of the 1970s Lusaka, Zambia, project the decision-making and planning of infrastructure layouts was undertaken collectively by each group of 25 households that shared a communal water-point and sanitary facility in the new settlement in which they were to be rehoused. This early stage of important decision-making was effectively used by community workers to develop a sense of collective identity and solidarity (Schlyter 1995). The Kuda-ki-Bustee project in Hyderabad, Pakistan, initiated in 1986 (see Case Study 4, p. 42), illustrated a somewhat more extreme 'hands-off' approach to service provision in which the residents decided the extent to which they were prepared to save in order to continue to install and upgrade infrastructure and services, for which they were eligible only after house construction by a majority of individual households had commenced, and for which they had to provide community labour. In several neighbourhood blocks collective funds, deposited for community service provision by plot beneficiaries, were accumulated in excess of their due instalments in order to speed and extend the development process (UNCHS 1991).

A common strategy for minimising the initial capital cost of infrastructure and services in urban S&S projects has been the application of the concept of incremental improvement to them as well as to the construction of dwellings. The rationale of this approach was that, whilst basic services had to be provided right from the beginning of a S&S project, they should be kept to a minimal provision of communal water points and pit-based sanitary facilities, unpaved roads, unlined surface water drains, etc. – to be upgraded over time in response to the development of community cohesion and demands and householders' increasing ability to pay for higher standards. However, as indicated above, despite the savings in initial cost there were drawbacks to this approach. Maintenance requirements were high when the sense of community was weakest, leading to neglect, rapid deterioration and vandalism; the public facilities did not help to instil a sense of local pride when it was most needed for community development and investment in house building; new neighbourhoods were launched with the stigma of being 'sub-standard'.

Where decisions on the levels and type of infrastructure provision had to be made without community consultation, it was a common mistake to assume that service standards should always have been low or that they, unlike the dwellings they served, necessarily had to be upgradeable over time. There are strong arguments in favour of providing high standards right from the start of an incremental housing project in order to stimulate good quality construction by individual house builders and a sense of pride in the neighbourhood in order to motivate local care and maintenance of public facilities (Cotton & Franceys 1991). Furthermore, in many contexts low-income neighbourhoods need relatively high standards of public open space and children's play areas, in part because of limited private dwelling space, particularly in cultures and climates that value social interaction through outdoor living. Also, security lighting, bus stop shelters and police posts all tend to be needed more than in upper- and middle-income group residential areas where insecurity usually tends to be less of an issue (UN-Habitat 2007). In addition, there is a strong moral argument and growing lobby for the principle that urban poor households have as much right to good quality public infrastructure and services as the better-off urban households (E&U 2015).

The cost of high standards of initial provision of infrastructure may be recovered in several ways such as long recovery periods linked to tariffs on user charges or spreading the cost beyond the confines of the project, through local (municipal) taxation schemes. It has been observed that the principle of 'full cost recovery' at the level of individual projects, espoused by aid agencies, notably the World Bank, in the 1970s and 1980s, disadvantaged the poor beneficiaries of many S&S and settlement upgrading projects, who were expected to bear the full capital cost of their neighbourhood infrastructure and service installations, whilst the cost of capital works in formal upper-income group urban neighbourhoods was spread across the city as a whole through the universal property tax system or levies on citywide user charges. Another approach to keeping the cost of infrastructure low has been by depending on community labour for construction work.[6] This has taken several forms ranging from the organisation of volunteer 'sweat equity' whereby project beneficiaries contribute their time and skills, to 'community contracting' in which a CBO forms a commercial company (usually with NGO managerial assistance) to tender for and undertake neighbourhood infrastructure works (Cotton & Sohail 1997). There are many variations in between, such as requiring formal sector commercial contractors to engage local labour in their workforces, a strategy as much aimed at income generation as minimising the cost of procurement of infrastructure. The highly successful participatory 'lane committees' very effectively serviced the big informal settlement of Orangi in Karachi, Pakistan, with virtually no public sector intervention (Hasan 2009).

Experience with such participatory approaches to the procurement of public infrastructure and services has varied widely in terms of the efficiency of the process, quality of the product and in the saving in capital cost. The looser forms of casual volunteering have worked well in upgrading projects where an established community existed and there was a strong sense of community solidarity and organisation (with strong leadership) and a locally perceived need for the improvement of infrastructure. In Aleppo, Syria, before the civil war, the occupants of several informal settlements successfully installed relatively sophisticated waterborne sewerage systems serving every dwelling[7] with no formal technical assistance and at no capital cost to the city government. However, where strong community ties do not already exist, as in many S&S projects, and where there has been an entrenched perception that the provision of infrastructure is 'the responsibility of government', attempts to mobilise voluntary labour and organise self-help have rarely been satisfactory or cost-saving and have on occasions led to bad political press and even to accusations of supporting exploitative unpaid 'slave-labour' practices. Nevertheless, in Ghana, for example, the Cooperative Housing Foundation recommended in 2002 that access to basic services in low-income group settlements should be largely through self-help efforts and the use of community builders, which seems to have been widely acceptable (CFH 2004).

In summary, the planning of infrastructure works has to be managed carefully. A lack of coordination between the various agencies responsible for infrastructure in S&S projects in the past has often led to delays in the provision of services and the installation of water supply and sanitation systems. Reduced service provision, as in the case of the Parcelles Assainies S&S project in Dakar, Senegal, referred to above (see Case Study 5, p. 47), stored up problems for the future and on occasions justified the fear of officials that the outcome of their projects were little better than slums. In that project, for example, cuts in the provision of education facilities and a lack of long-term planning meant that on its completion there were only 22 public primary schools with up to 80 children per classroom for a primary school age population of 87,000 (Cohen 2007).

8.4 Beneficiary Selection

The selection of beneficiaries of support to incremental housing projects presents a plethora of conflicting priorities, indicators, political patronage and potential for corruption.

Technically, the support given to upgrading existing informal settlements has been most successful when it was in response to a rational and transparent hierarchy of priorities based on (GIS) indicators of degrees of 'housing stress' and potential 'returns on investment', as in the Favela Bairro programme in Rio de Janeiro, Brazil, described in Section 4.2. Of course, a complex range of political pressures invariably influences the 'rationality' of any such approach, but it should not negate it. Whilst the physical aspects of 'housing stress' are relatively easy to appraise, social and economic indicators that can be addressed by slum upgrading have been less easy to appraise. Similarly the potential 'returns on investment' embrace a complex web of social costs and sustainable benefits in addition to physical and sustainable environmental gains.

Incremental housing projects are likely to fall into one of two broad categories: (1) those for rehousing existing urban communities that have to be relocated; and (2) 'open access' projects in which any eligible household may individually apply for a plot. In the first of these, beneficiary selection is in theory relatively straightforward. Those who have been evicted from their previous dwelling or have had to abandon their homes as a result of disaster, receive a plot and whatever other compensation that is agreed. However, invariably there are winners and losers in this process, not only within the relocated community but also beyond it. For instance, the victims of disasters have often ended up better off than many who were seemingly 'more deserving' but not affected by the disaster. This is a general dilemma, not specifically related to the beneficiaries of incremental housing programmes and projects.

Eligibility criteria for the selection of beneficiaries for 'open access' projects are generally based on household income levels and assets and other indicators of housing need. Defining and justifying such criteria can be difficult and has often led to excessively complicated application and verification procedures that are cumbersome to administer. The Kudu-ki-Bastee project in Hyderabad, Pakistan, described in Case Study 4, overcame such complications through a stringent process of self-selection and 'flooding the market' with small plots in order to satisfy demand. However, this process excluded many less desperate and less able low-income families who were left to fend for themselves in the informal sector (Hasan 2000).

Thus while administration should be kept to a minimum and controls should be as flexible as possible, restrictions may have to be imposed in order to ensure that government-supported incremental housing does not primarily benefit middle-income groups, or others with affordable access to the formal private sector housing market. In Senegal's S&S programme, (see Case Study 5, p. 47), measures taken against speculation included prohibiting the sale of plots for five years after occupation plus a levy for changing ownership that brought the total plot cost higher than the purchase price of land in the open market (ENDA-RUP 2005). In the context of its work in Central America, SIDA found that migration was changing the way in which its partners had to work, requiring shifts in conventional definitions of the household and eligibility criteria, with fixed abode, proof of residency and income verification all increasingly difficult to obtain, thus demanding new more flexible (and perhaps less accountable) approaches to beneficiary selection (SIDA 2007).

In the past, some S&S projects have been designed to accommodate a range of different low- and middle-income beneficiaries and to make plots available on the open market in order to encourage a social/income group mix of population thereby hoping to avoid 'single-class' neighbourhoods and in some cases to use the sale of up-market plots to subsidise those for the lower income groups. In many cases these objectives have been met. However, they have proved to be difficult to administer and prone to exploitation. In the Dandora project in Nairobi, Kenya, a range different plot sizes were designed for a corresponding range of eligible income groups (see Case Study 3, p. 41). The subletting of rooms was encouraged to supplement household incomes and provide accommodation for families who were not willing or able to get on the property ownership ladder. However, it was found that the lower income householders tended to be squeezed out of the subletting market by the better-off owners many of whom developed their larger plots exclusively for commercial letting (Lee-Smith and Memon 1988).

In summary, beneficiary selection for 'open-access' incremental housing projects is inevitably a delicate process that invariably involves both commercial and political interests. Because of this, every effort has had to be made to develop clear indicators, transparent procedures and accountable management processes. Projects for the resettlement of established informal settlement communities is somewhat easier, particularly as the selection and plot allocation process that can, and should be, undertaken in close collaboration with the beneficiary community and its leaders, if not exclusively by them. It is envisaged that such a process, whereby a community of 'settlers', probably organised and led by NGOs, will, as organised collectives, enter partnership arrangements for identifying appropriately located land (within the confines of official master plan zoning, and other citywide development control legislation) and its development as new incrementally developed city neighbourhoods. In many cities, this will require a new type of proactive NGOs[8] and novel types of negotiating arrangements and partnerships between them and municipal governments and administrations.

8.5 Site Planning, Building Controls and Supports

Site planning almost invariably has to be undertaken as a centrally controlled technical service, though on a micro level it has occasionally been done with the participation of the project beneficiaries as in the 1970s Lusaka, Zambia, project in which communities of 25 households made decisions on the distribution of land area between public and private use and local houseplot layouts around their centralised common sanitary facilities (Jere 1984).

The distribution of land uses, plot sizes and access layouts will normally be determined by prevailing municipal norms and regulations. However, as indicated in Section 3.1, S&S projects, which tended to be treated as 'experimental' exercises, were often used to test and/or demonstrate the rationalisation (reduction) of excessively generous statutory planning standards, whilst maintaining adequate and socially acceptable, conditions of health, safety and amenity. The Sri Lanka MHP, described in Section 4.1, is an example.

Allowing for mixed land use, both at the outset of incremental housing projects and in their subsequent development, is an important principle that applies to all low-income settlements. The extent to which low-income groups depend on home-based industries for their livelihoods and for their integration into the urban economy at large is becoming well understood (Tipple 2004). The provision of dedicated workshop space within settlements is similarly important and invariably used by local residents, as had been described in the context of the Shivaji Park project in Alwar, India (Lall 2002).

Planning and building standards also tend to present problems. Unable to breakaway, either psychologically or legally, from long-established and unrealistic planning and building codes, government officers on occasions have sought to impose unnecessarily, and unaffordably, high standards on S&S projects, for example, large plot sizes, mandatory standard house designs, high-cost construction materials and low residential densities. Some S&S schemes have even attempted to prohibit income-generating activities on residential plots, including the renting of rooms, thereby limiting the opportunities for residents to earn an (additional) income to help cover the costs that they have to pay for their plot and their house.

Planning for higher densities of land use can also reduce costs. For example, in 2000 smaller plot sizes were recommended as part of a planning reform programme in Ghana with the intention of reducing the cost of servicing land by achieving greater economies of scale and enabling the development of smaller infill sites in developed urban areas that were already served by trunk infrastructure (CHF 2004). Changing building codes to enable multiple additional floors to be added over time can increase densities considerably (as seen in Dakar) but this should be achieved without compromising safety, especially in earthquake prone areas (World Bank 2015). High-rise incremental housing is also a possibility, as demonstrated by the Ciudad Bachué project in Bogotá, Colombia, in the 1970s (see Case Study 8b, p. 55), but can prove demanding in relation to long-term expansion and the maintenance of structural safety.

As has been stressed in earlier chapters, building controls should be confined to those necessary to ensure the health, safety and amenity of households and the wider community and facilitate incremental construction processes. Many early S&S projects were not successful because their target groups could not afford the cost of meeting the conditions set for their development. The Dandora project in Nairobi, Kenya, required at least two rooms to be completed using permanent materials (i.e. concrete or dressed stone for walls) within 24 months of plot allocation (Lee Smith & Memon 1988). By contrast, in the Kuda-ki-Bustee scheme in Pakistan, the Hyderabad Development Authority deliberately sought to free householders from planning controls. Only the site layout of the project's neighbourhoods was fixed and absolutely no standards were imposed on the plan or quality of the houses built on each plot (Siddiqui 2005). It was rightly assumed that self-builders are conservative and risk averse, tending not to want to experiment with new construction materials and methods. They naturally aspire to high standards and would not willfully build their dwellings in ways that might make them unsafe or a threat to the health of their families. However, to achieve this they needed technical information and advice and on how to evolve their homes, often over quite long periods of time, which was largely provided by NGOs (see Case Study 4, p. 42).

In summary, revised planning and building codes and procedures to support self-builders are needed in many countries. These should be pro-scriptive, setting the performance limits of good practice, rather than the more common prescriptive legislation that stipulates in some detail what has to be done, leaving little room for innovation. Good outreach is essential for households to be able to make informed and technically sound choices and to ensure that they achieve value for money. Thus there are strong arguments for a shift from the concept of official development control to 'develop-ment promotion' and the establishment of planning and building advisory services for incremental housing programmes and projects that provide technical guidance on good practice. A 'building clinic', that performed this function was set up and staffed by architecture and engineering students in the vast Thawra City (later known as Sadr City) incremental housing project in Baghdad, Iraq, for a short time in the early 1970s (Wakely et al. 1974). Some NGO-run urban resource centres have provided this sort of on-site technical assistance to low-income group house builders.[9] However, there is still a need for development control functions to police illegal develop-ment and unsafe building by unscrupulous speculators. Squatting on land reserved for service buildings or public open space has frequently occurred. Speculators building accommodation for subletting, with a view to max-imising profits, tend to have little regard for the quality of construction, to the extent that low-income rental housing constructed for this purpose in official S&S projects as well as in informal settlements has been physi-cally unsafe, particularly in earthquake-prone areas and those impacted by climate change (UN-Habitat 2011; World Bank 2015).

Ideally, the primary functions of development control policing should be undertaken by the community of residents, though enforcement must remain the responsibility of the state. Whilst NGOs may be best placed to provide neighbourhood-level planning and building advisory services and to build CBO capacity to administer first-stage development control functions, it is important that government has the capacity to ensure their complicity.

8.6 Community Organisation and Asset Management

The importance of a sense of 'ownership' of local community facilities that engenders a degree of collective responsibility for their maintenance and management by the community is now well understood. What is often less clear is the link between 'ownership' and the participation of households in all stages of the project planning process. Few of the upgrading and resettlement projects of the 1970s and 1980s engaged with people, least of all at the appraisal and planning stages of pre-project implementation. User needs and demands for land and services were assumed with little or no consultation (with the notable exception of the Lusaka upgrading and S&S project referred to above (Jere 1984)). In new 'open access' incremental housing projects where the beneficiaries are not identified until after the site planning stage such participation is obviously not possible, so support to community building with an emphasis on the new and developing environment should be a high priority right from first days of occupation. The administration of the Dandora S&S project in Nairobi, Kenya, was centred on the Community Development Department especially established for the project (Lee Smith & Memon 1988). In the Kuda-ki-Bustee project in Pakistan (see Case Study 4, p. 42) the most successful neighbourhoods in terms of developing and maintaining public infrastructure and services were those that received NGO community development and management support right from the first days of settlement (Hasan 2000).

Over time community-based management organisations have developed to cater for local collective needs. In Dakar, for instance, insufficient infrastructure was installed and there was no planning for the future growth of the settlement, but cultural and religious organisations that developed within the community gradually built the capacities required to deal with the area's deficits in education and healthcare facilities, garbage collection and sewage disposal (Cohen 2007). But this was a slow process that, with more support in the initial stages of the project would probably have been more effective.

In short, it is essential that the capacity to support local organisations in the management and maintenance of community assets is essential right from the start of the incremental development process. In most cases this entails careful educative processes that in the long run lead to permanent local governance structures (Max Locke Centre 2005). Clearly these should be targeted around specific issues and user groups – parents' associations concerned with school facilities; street or local area committees concerned with the maintenance of neighbourhood roads, access paths and drains – the membership and roles of which will change as the incremental development process evolves.

8.7 The Private Sector

The formal private sector in some countries has had an effective role in the installation of infrastructure and service delivery through conventional subcontracting arrangements in both settlement upgrading and S&S projects. Virtually all official agencies, throughout the world, are legally required to contract formally registered companies or operate through recognised NGOs. Community groups and individual households, however, are at liberty to employ informal contractors who are not constrained by the obligations of 'formality' (conditions of employment, quality control, capital recovery, tax obligations, etc.), giving them a commercial advantage over their formal sector competitors.

Not only is the formal private sector's involvement in low-income development inhibited by its commercial disadvantage, it also tends to be intimidated by perceptions of the high risk of such involvement, stoked by the, generally erroneous, reputation of 'slums' and low-income communities as harbingers of crime and extortion. Nevertheless, there are opportunities for formal sector enterprises to participate productively in incremental housing development processes, particularly those that are prepared to respond to the often relatively slow, irregular and unpredictable nature of incremental development by low-income communities and households.

An interesting example of incremental service delivery by the private sector is the *aguateros* of Asunción in Paraguay, who were medium- or small-scale entrepreneurs who, in the 1990s, provided potable pipe-born water to some 400,000 inhabitants of low-income group settlements (approximately 17 per cent of all connections in the city) that would otherwise not be served by the municipal supply system. Anticipating the informal, or officially sanctioned, occupation of peri-urban land, an *aguatero* would sink a borehole and start to extend a polythene pipe network, making connections to client house plots at costs that were comparable to the subsidised official public sector suppliers. They also provided credit to client householders on mutually agreed terms to meet their costs. A typical *aguatero* served up to around 100 customers on a single borehole. They were subject to official water quality certification every six months that guaranteed their safety and constancy of supply. *Aguateros* joined forces and created an association to protect their interests, strengthen their public image and prevent attempts by the large utility companies to drive them out of business (MIT 2001).

Another innovative example of the formal private sector, in this case, specifically addressing the construction needs of low-income group incremental house-builder families is that of the Mexican cement and construction materials conglomerate, Cemex, through its *Patrimonio Hoy* programme. This was a commercially profit-making scheme in which householders paid approximately US$14 per week over a period of 70 weeks for which they received architectural and engineering advice and building materials for the construction or extension of their dwellings, delivered to their properties at stable prices as and when they were needed. If a family's fortunes changed, so that it could not make payments or store or use building materials, they could 'pause' the process and 'bank' their materials. In the decade following its start in 2000, Patrimonio Hoy was subscribed to by over 250,000 low-income households to construct 160,000 c. 10 m^2 rooms to a total value of US$135million with a default rate on payments of less than 1 per cent. Patrimonio Hoy beneficiaries consistently claimed that their building was easier, cheaper and of better quality than if it had been done on their own. Cemex benefited from a previously untapped market, creating solid and expanding 'brand loyalty' and exploiting the company's reputation for social responsibility (Business in the Community 2010).

A third area of private sector engagement in affordable urbanisation, though not specifically confined to incremental development, lies in the complexities of land markets for low-income group housing. Universally, there is a blurring of boundaries between formal and informal dealings in land and the role of agents and brokers in land and property title transfers. An interesting solution to the dilemma of the conflict between affordability and legality is provided by Argoz, a private sector developer in San Salvador, El Salvador in the late 1970s. Argoz identified and purchased privately owned peri-urban land at agricultural prices, subdivided it and let plots on a ten-year rent-to-own basis to householders with monthly incomes of c. US$170. Payments ranged from US$5–20 per month, depending on a mutually agreed amortisation period. In addition, Argoz provided purchasers with design and technical advice and helped secure the provision of public urban infrastructure and services. In the 23 years to 2000, over 300,000 low-income group households had obtained secure title to affordable properties and Argoz' assets had grown from US$50,000 to over $140 million. In 1998, the mayor of Bogotá, Colombia, established 'MetroVivienda', a municipal agency (quango) to operate on a similar basis to Argoz in San Salvador (Ferguson & Navarete 2003).

In summary, the formal private sector has attributes of managerial expertise, access to capital and commercial networks that can contribute to low-income group incremental housing processes. However, in many urbanising countries, particularly those where the indigenous private sector is weak, it has not seen the opportunities presented by low-income group housing development, or has shied away from the perceived risks. Thus, its role has tended to remain on the safe ground of government contracts that do not require great entrepreneurial initiatives. Where they have innovated, as in the examples described above, there is significant evidence of win-win outcomes that can benefit both low-income group households and communities and private sector enterprises, though such strategies have to be entertained with some caution as the private sector's profit-driven objectives differ significantly from those of most low-income group communities and the public sector and civil society institutions that support them and there are potential risks of extortion.

8.8 Strategic Planning

For state-supported incremental housing initiatives to have a significant impact on the enormous low-income housing deficits of most cities and towns, they must be located within a broader framework. At the national level there needs to be a clear poverty reduction strategy that recognises the detrimental significance of urban poverty on national and regional development and the role that urban housing can play in reducing it (Gattoni 2009). At the level of the city, small-scale incremental housing projects that are divorced from the wider housing market can become subject to speculation and rapid gentrification. This was the case in Dakar, Senegal (see Case Study 5, p. 47), where plots were quickly sold on to higher income groups because these groups had no safer investment opportunities (Cohen 2007). The same problem is also evidenced in Pakistani cities, where during the 1990s higher income groups bought plots intended for low-income housing development as a hedge against inflation (Hasan 2000). By contrast, in Shivaji Park in Alwar, India, one of the reasons for the high retention rate of original low-income residents in the project was the fairly balanced housing market of Alwar (Lall 2002). Unfortunately, most urban housing markets are far from fairly balanced.

In the early 2000s, it was recommended that the government of Ghana should develop non-conventional strategies for four different market segments to improve housing supply and finance for each. It was also argued that within each sector there were differentiated groups of developers, households and communities, each of which drove housing supply and therefore comprehensive strategies should involve all of these actors. It was recommended that components of the strategy should include projects for the high- and upper-middle-income market that maximise the use of local building materials and formal sector borrowing. Recommendations were also made for the provision of S&S for lower-middle and low-income groups, informal settlement upgrading and promoting wholesale lending between commercial banks, state banks and microfinance institutions (CHF 2004).

Situating low-income group incremental housing initiatives firmly within the context of broader City Development Strategies (CDSs), discussed in Section 6.1, and land management reforms and programmes to facilitate housing supply for all income groups is an essential component of their long-term success and their potential to have an impact on city development at a significant scale.

Notes

1 For example Nairobi, Kenya; Johannesburg, South Africa; Phnom Penh, Cambodia; Ahmedabad, India and many places besides.
2 This is a partnership between the NSDF, Mahila Milan (Women Together) coalition of urban CBOs in India and SPARC, a Mumbai-based NGO.
3 See: http://unhabitat.org/GLTN/
4 This section draws upon UN-Habitat (2005) and UN-ESCAP (1991). See also: E&U (2007, 2008).
5 Infrastructure refers to: water supply networks; neighbourhood sanitation (sewerage) system; electric power supply system; vehicular and pedestrian access ways (roads and footpaths) and vehicle parking places; surface water drainage; street lighting; solid waste collection points, etc.; public open (recreation/sports) spaces. Services are: education, health, security and cultural and recreation services and facilities and buildings and related open spaces (schools; clinics/health posts; police stations/posts; markets; community centres; religious facilities/buildings; libraries; etc.).
6 'Voluntary' community labouring has been an important political pillar of local development and solidarity in many countries, e.g. the Ujamaa movements in Tanzania and Kenya in the 1960s and 1970s and the Sarvodaya Shramadana movement in Sri Lanka in the same period.
7 Notably, the large informal settlements of Sheikh Maqsoud and Ashrafeyeh in the North West of Aleppo.
8 i.e. able to operate in similar, though legal, ways to the political organisations that have been engaged in the mobilisation and organisation of squatters' land invasions in the past, such as the Colombian Communist Party's role in the invasion and settlement of Barrio Policarpa in Bogotá, Colombia, in 1966, described in Section 1.2.
9 For example, OPP Research and Training Institute and Urban Resource Centre, Pakistan (Hasan 2009), Sevanatha Urban Resource Centre, Sri Lanka and Phnom Penh Urban Resource Centre (URC), Cambodia.

References

ACHR, 2004, 'Negotiating the right to stay in the city', *Environment & Urbanization*, Vol. 16, No. 1, Sage, London, UK.
Angel, S. & T. Chirathamkijkul, 1983, 'Slum reconstruction: Land sharing as an alternative to eviction in Bangkok', in Angel, S. (eds) *Land for Housing the Poor*, Select Books, Singapore.
Bakhtyar, B., A. Zaharim, K. Sopiam & S. Moghimi, 2013, *Housing for Poor People: A Review on Low-Cost Housing Process in Malaysia*, WSEAS Transactions on Environment & Development. Online at: www.wseas.org/multimedia/journals/environment/2013/5715–106.pdf
Business in the Community, 2010, "case studies'. Online at: www..btc.org.uk/resources/case_studies

CHF, 2004, *Strategic Assessment of the Affordable Housing Sector in Ghana*, CHF International, Silver Spring, MD, USA.

Cohen, M., 2007, 'Aid, density and urban form: Anticipating Dakar', *Built Environment*, Vol. 33, No. 2, Alexandrine Press, Oxford, UK.

Cotton, A. & R. Franceys, 1991, *Services for Shelter*, Liverpool Planning Manual 3, Liverpool University Press, Liverpool, UK.

Cotton, A. & M. Sohail, 1997, 'Community partnered procurement: A socially sensitive option', *Waterlines: International Journal of Appropriate Technologies for Water Supply and Sanitation*, Vol. 16, No. 2, ITDG Publishing, Rugby, UK.

D'Monte, D. (ed.) 2006, *Mills for Sale: The Way Ahead*, Marg Publications, Mumbai, India.

ENDA-RUP, 2005, *Parcelles Assainie*. Online at: www.hicnet.org/document. php?pid=2611

E&U, 2007, 'Finance for low-income housing and community development', *Environment & Urbanization*, Vol. 19, No. 2, Sage, London, UK.

E&U, 2008, 'Finance for housing, livelihoods and basic services', *Environment & Urbanization*, Vol. 20, No. 1, Sage, London, UK.

E&U, 2009, 'Getting land for housing: What strategies work for low-income groups?', *Environment & Urbanization Brief*, No. 19, London, UK.

E&U, 2015, 'Sanitation and drainage in cities', *Environment & Urbanization*, Vol. 27, Nos. 1 and 2, Sage, London, UK.

Ferguson, B. & J. Navarete, 2003, 'A financial framework for reducing slums: Lessons from experience in Latin America', *Environment & Urbanization*, Vol. 15, No. 2, Sage, London, UK.

Gattoni, G., 2009, 'A case for the incremental housing in sites-and-services programs', paper presented at IDB conference, July. Online at: http://idbdocs.iadb. org/WSDocs/getDocument.aspx?DOCNUM-2062811

GoSL (Government of Sri Lanka), 1983, *Housing Options and Loans Package (HOLP): Million Houses Programme*, National Housing Development Authority, Colombo, Sri Lanka.

Hamdi, N. & R. Goethert, 1997, *Action Planning for Cities: A Guide to Community Practice*, John Ailey & Sons, Chichester, UK.

Hasan, A., 2000, *Housing for the Poor: Failure of Formal Sector Strategies*, City Press, Karachi, Pakistan.

Hasan, A., 2009, *Participatory Development: The Story of the Orangi Pilot Project – Research and Training Institute and Urban Resource Centre, Karachi*, Oxford University Press, Oxford, UK.

Jere, H., 1984, 'Lusaka: Local participation in planning and decision-making', in Payne, G.K. (ed.) *Low Income Housing in the Developing World: The Role of Sites and Services and Settlement Upgrading*, Wiley, Chichester, UK.

Keivani, R., M. Mattingly & H. Majedi, 2008, 'Public management of urban land, enabling markets and low income housing provision: the overlooked experience of Iran', *Urban Studies*, Vol. 45, No. 9, Sage, London, UK.

Lall, S., 2002, 'An evaluation of a public sector low income housing project in Alwar: India', *Working Paper 6*, Society for Development Studies, New Delhi, India.

Lee-Smith, D. & Memon, P., 1988, 'Institution development for delivery of low-income housing: An evaluation of Dandora Community Development Project in Nairobi', *Third World Planning Review*, Vol. 10 No. 3, Liverpool, UK.

Lewis, M. & P. Conaty, 2012, *The Resilience Imperative: Cooperative Transitions to a Steady State Economy*, New Society, Gabriola Island, BC, Canada.

Max Locke Centre, 2005, *The Rough Guide to Community Asset Management*, MLC Press, University of Westminster, London, UK.

McAuslan, P., 1985, *Urban Land and Shelter for the Poor*, Earthscan, London, UK.

MIT, 2001, 'Upgrading urban communities: a resource for urban practitioners'. Online at: http://web.mit.edu/urbanupgrading/index.html

Patel, S. & D. Mitlin, 2004, 'The work of SPARC, the National Slum Dwellers Federation and Mahila Milan', in Mitlin, D. & D. Satterthwaite (eds) *Empowering Squatter Citizens: The Roles of Local Governments and Civil Society in Reducing Urban Poverty*, Earthscan, London, UK.

Payne, G.K., A. Durand-Lasserve & C. Rakodi, 2009, 'The limits to land titling and home ownership', *Environment & Urbanization*, Vol. 21, No. 2, Sage, London.

Rahman, M., 2005, 'Role of NGOs in urban housing for the poor in Dhaka, Bangladesh', *Global Built Environment Review*, Vol. 15, No. 1.

Schlyter, A., 1995, 'Squatter and slum settlements in Zambia', in Aldrich, B. & R. Sandhu (eds) *Housing the Urban Poor: Policy and Practice in Developing Countries*, Zed Books, London, UK.

SIDA, 2007, *Increasing Access to Housing and Financial Services: SIDA Experiences in Central America*, First Asia-Pacific Housing Forum, Singapore.

Siddiqui, T.A., 2005, *Incremental Housing Development Scheme (Pakistan): An Innovative and Successful Scheme for Sheltering the Urban Poor*, Action Research for Shelter, Karachi, Pakistan.

Stein, A. & I. Vance, 2008, 'The role of housing finance in addressing the needs of the urban poor: Lessons from Central America', *Environment & Urbanization*, Vol. 20, No. 1, Sage, London, UK.

Tipple, G., 2004, 'Settlement upgrading and home-based enterprises: Discussions from empirical data', *Cities*, Vol. 21, No. 5, Elsevier, Amsterdam, Netherlands.

Turner, J.F.C., 1976, *Housing by People: Towards Autonomy in Building Environments*, Marion Boyars, London, UK.

UN-ESCAP, 1991, *Guidelines on Community-based Housing Finance and Innovative Credit Systems for Low-income Households*, Economic and Social Commission for Asia and the Pacific, Bangkok, Thailand.

UN-Habitat, 2005, *Financing Urban Shelter: Global Report on Human Settlements 2005*, Earthscan, London, UK.

UN-Habitat, 2011, *Cities and Climate Change: Global Report on Human Settlements 2011*, Earthscan, London, UK.

UNCHS, 1991, *The Incremental Development Scheme: A Case Study of Kuda-Ki-Bustee in Hyderabad, Pakistan*, UNCHS Training Materials Series No. HS/232/91E, UN-Habitat, Nairobi, Kenya.

Van der Linden, J., 1992, 'Back to the roots: Keys to successful implementation of sites-and-services', in Mathéy, K. (ed.) *Beyond Self-Help Housing*, Mansell Publishing, London, UK.

Wakely, P., H. Schmetzer & B.Mumtaz, 1974, 'A building clinic in Baghdad', *Architectural Design*, No. 6 (74), London, UK.

Wakely, P., 2008, *Land Tenure in Under-Served Settlements in Colombo, Sri Lanka*, IDRC Poverty and Environment Report Series No.6, Ottawa, Canada.

World Bank, 2015, *Building Regulation for Resilience: Managing Risks for Safer Cities*, World Bank, Washington DC, USA.

9 Some Conclusions, Capacity Building and the Way Forward

Experience and analysis has demonstrated the efficiency and efficacy of incremental housing for and by urban low-income households and communities, supported by, and in partnership with local government. John Turner coined the phrase 'housing as a verb' (Turner 1972) to focus attention on the *processes* by which urban low-income families house themselves, and away from the prevailing preoccupation with housing solely as a *product*. Yet, four decades later this understanding had still not been absorbed by many national and municipal housing authorities that persisted with 'conventional' attitudes to the clearance of 'slums' and the unrealisable ambition to replace them with ready-built public housing. As a result urban informal (illegal) settlements in many towns and cities continued to expand (UN-Habitat 2003).

The principle of subsidiarity, set out in Section 3.2, and the empowerment of low-income communities and households are often not understood or are resisted because they are erroneously perceived to undermine the authority of established political interest groups.

However, in many situations the dominant constraint to devolving responsibility for the production, maintenance and management of affordable housing is the lack of appropriate technical and professional resources, rather than necessarily the failure of the political will to devolve. It is more a problem of 'enabling' than one of 'empowering' (see Section 3.2).

9.1 Capacity Building

To many, capacity building means only training or human resource development. Certainly this is a very major component of it. However, if decision-makers, managers, professionals and technicians are to operate at full capacity, they need more than just their own abilities. They need an institutional and organisational environment conducive to, and supportive of, their efforts, energies and skills. Institutional and organisational constraints present as great an impediment to the effective management of supports to incremental housing processes as the inabilities of professionals, technicians and householders. Therefore to be effective capacity building must simultaneously embrace all three aspects – human resource development, organisational development and institutional development.

Human Resource Development

Human resource development is the process of equipping individuals with the understanding, skills and the access to information and knowledge that enable them to perform effectively. Because of the often-unpredictable nature of devolved informal settlement upgrading or the participatory development of new housing, the traditional boundaries between professional and technical disciplines (architecture, planning, engineering, community development, etc.) have tended to become blurred and overlap. Interdependent multi-disciplinary teamwork is essential. Therefore, in addition to acquiring new skills that are needed to support incremental housing approaches in their own discipline, managers and technical professionals must also acquire a broad understanding of the full range of issues and activities outlined in Chapter 8 concerning: land; finance; infrastructure and services; beneficiary selection; planning and building controls; community organisation and asset management; and city-scale strategic planning.

At the start of the Sri Lanka Million Houses Programme in 1983, the National Housing Development Authority had to retrain and 're-tool' its entire decentralised professional and technical staff. Construction managers became the directors of support and supply teams providing advice, finance and building materials to community-based endeavours; housing officers became the field administrators of incremental loan funds; technical officers became the supervisors and trainers of household and community building processes. This was largely a learning-by-doing-and-sharing process of capacity building that included the development of new job descriptions, formal training, and the opening of new career opportunities (Lankatilleke 1986).

Organisational Development

Organisational development is the process by which things get done collectively within an organisation, be it a central government ministry, a local authority department, a private sector enterprise, a non-governmental organisation (NGO) or community group. It is to do with management practices and procedures; rules and regulations; hierarchies and job descriptions – *how things get done*. It is also to do with working relationships; shared goals and values; teamwork, dependencies and supports – *why things get done*. In many situations flexible and responsive management styles are needed, requiring entirely new organisational structures, particularly within local government. It also often calls for the establishment of new relationships between different organisations, for example those responsible for poverty reduction programmes, community development, environmental health, adult education, enhancing the roles and opportunities for women, that hitherto have had little engagement with housing departments or authorities.

As described in Section 3.2, in 1975 Nairobi City Council in Kenya established a special new Project Department (upgraded to a permanent Housing Development Department (HDD) in 1978) to design and manage the Dandora sites and services (S&S) project to the east of the city (see Case Study 3, p. 41). The creation of a whole new department was deemed necessary because the management and professional skills and relationships that were required differed significantly from those of the Council's existing Housing and Social Services Department and other related departments, notably Engineering and Water and Sewerage. A pivotal component of the HDD was its Community Development Division that took on functions and professionals that had not existed in the city administration before. The HDD built its own capacity as it developed with considerable success – again, learning-by-doing – even though political rivalries between the new organisation and the longer-established City Council departments to some extent obstructed its operation in the early stages (Lee-Smith & Memon 1988). The devolution of authority, redesignation of technical and professional skills, and the retraining required to implement the devolved Million Houses Programme in Sri Lanka is described in Section 4.1.

Institutional Development

Institutional development encompasses the legal and regulatory changes that have to be made in order to enable organisations and agencies at all levels and in all sectors to enhance their capacities. It embraces such issues as: regulations controlling the financial management and the borrowing and trading capacity of government agencies and municipal authorities; the ability of local government to negotiate contracts and form partnerships with private enterprises and community organisations; land management, tenure and use regulations; statutory building standards and other development controls; and democratic legislation that allows, enables and encourages communities to take responsibility for the management of their own neighbourhoods and services. Such institutional and legal issues generally need the political and legislative authority of national government to bring about effective changes.

In 2006–2007 the Ministry of Urban Development in Afghanistan was in a situation of radical change having been divested of many of its former responsibilities. The minister saw this as an opportunity to turn the ministry into 'an organisation that enables municipalities, urban districts and communities to plan and manage their environmental, economic, social and housing development in a participatory and coordinated way'. That is, to turn the Ministry into an advisory and capacity building organisation. However, to do this required a level of constitutional change involving the agreement of the President and Cabinet and the rewriting of inter-ministerial relationships, notably those of the Ministry of the Interior that was responsible for local government.

The City Statute promulgated by the federal government of Brazil in 2001, supported by a new Ministry of Cities and National Cities Council, established two years later, provided a 'toolbox' of legal instruments that enabled municipal governments to manage their own affairs within the tenets of Brazil's progressive 1988 national constitution. Emphasis was given to the social use of urban land with a particular focus on informal settlements and the land needs of low-income households and communities. Though, at the beginning the City Statute was subjected to some political opposition from entrenched conservative interest groups at all levels, there is little question that it had a significant impact at the urban grassroots level. Processes such as municipal participatory budgeting, the regularisation of tenure to land and property in informal settlements, state-private sector-civil society partnerships in urban development and management were enabled by legislation emanating from it (Fernandes 2010).

Priorities

As emphasised above, capacity needs to be built at every level and across all fields of activity that impinge upon the development and management of cities and settlements. However, in every situation there are priorities that, for reasons of urgency or deficiency, take precedent over others in their need for attention and resources. These vary with the particular circumstances of any specific country or region. Nevertheless, it has become increasingly apparent that the weakest link in the chain is generally at the level of local government and municipal administration.

Municipal governments and administrations are the key actors in the management of towns and cities. Yet, in all but a handful of countries, they have been starved of authority and resources. They have tended to be constrained by obsolete legislation, restrictive practices, outmoded equipment and inappropriately trained staff. Many of their traditional development and management roles have been usurped or bypassed by central government corporations and utility companies. Also, in many cities some of their customary roles have also been rendered redundant by the innovative NGOs and low-income households and communities that they have failed to serve. But the paradigms are changing and, at the beginning of the twenty-first century are calling for an urgent and massive exercise in rebuilding the capacity of local government and administration, including their capacity to provide appropriate supports to the development of low-income group incremental housing (McCarney 1996).

Community-based organisations (CBOs) and local NGOs rank close to formal local government in the league of priorities for capacity building in support of incremental housing processes. The emerging role of neighbourhood and community groups, as a new tier of local governance that comes between individual households and municipal authorities, is almost without precedent. Although urban community organisations are rightly taking on many of the traditional grassroots management functions of municipal authorities with which they are in partnership, it is important that they remain 'non-governmental' so that they can maintain an independent 'watchdog' role over municipal authorities, holding them to account and guarding the demands and interests of their constituents (Bebbington et al. 2008).

The private sector that, by definition, is only in the game to make a profit, generally takes responsibility for building and maintaining its own capacity to compete. There are situations, however, where the informal private sector and some formal sector small- and medium-sized enterprises need assistance in the form of specific and precisely targeted legislative deregulation and incentives that encourage and enable them to enter the market for the production of low-cost housing and infrastructure. In many situations there is also the need for easy access to management training for small and informal sector enterprises. This is often as much in the interests of their clients as their own competitive ability.

9.2 In Conclusion – The Way Ahead

Almost half the population of the developing world live and work in towns and cities and a third of them (830 million) in informal settlements or slums (UN-Habitat 2003). Though there are many 'slums of despair' – seemingly hopeless neighbourhoods of endemic poverty and environmental degradation – the majority are 'settlements of hope' – informal neighbourhoods and communities in the process of building their homes and neighbourhoods and thereby their cities through their own endeavours and ingenuity. As described in Chapter 1, they demonstrate a process that has been shown to be both effective and efficient in terms of its responsiveness to its participants' fluctuating needs and fortunes. However, they are often constrained by a lack of officially recognised supports that would extend the efficiency and efficacy of incremental housing processes to the development of the city as a whole.

A key attribute to the success of informal urban housing development processes that distinguish them from the constraints of formal housing procurement is the location-based value of land and, therefore, its cost (Madden & Marcuse 2016) for which they do not pay; the land in informal settlements is free, or at a cost well below its formal private sector 'market' price.

Since the beginning of the twenty-first century there has been an increasing move towards returning land to the status of a 'social common' – separating it from the status and value of the developments upon it, or improvements to it, in the transition to a 'steady state', interest-free, economy (Lewis & Conaty 2012).

Emphasis has been given to the importance of NGOs as key links between formal local government and administration and individual households and community leaders, and as educated advisers and managers of local urban development and management processes. However, as global and local economies and societies continue to develop, it is likely that the importance of this mediation will diminish and ultimately become obsolete, being replaced by the accumulation and free exchange of knowledge and information within and directly between urban low-income housing partnerships[1] (Mason 2016).

The starting point for the process of developing direct interface and partnership engagement between public sector agencies and organised urban low-income groups is the understanding and application of the principle of subsidiarity and the political will to devolve authority through all levels and fields of decision-making and action, coupled with investment in innovative, integrated capacity building in each level and field of operation in the process of introducing incremental social and public housing policies and implementation strategies through authentic co-production partnerships.

Note

1 The federalisation' and 'globalisation' of urban low-income group housing-related CBO-local authority partnerships started in the 1980s. The Asian Coalition for housing Rights (ACHR) was established in 1988. By 2014, through its Asian Coalition for Community Action (ACCA) programme, its network embraced supports to more than 1,100 low-income group housing development projects of various sizes and degrees of complexity in 165 cities in 19 Asian countries. Shack/Slum Dwellers International (SDI) was inaugurated in 1996 as a network of low-income group housing CBO federations, which by 2016 had 33 national affiliates, organised in regional 'hubs' in East, Southern and West Africa, Asia and emerging in Latin America.

References

Bebbington, A., S, Hickey & D. Mitlin (eds), 2008, *Can NGOs Make a Difference? The Challenge of Development Alternatives*, Zed Books Ltd, London, UK and New York, USA

Fernandes, E., 2010, 'The City Statute and the legal urban order', in Cities Alliance, The City Statute of Brazil: A Commentary, Cities Alliance, Washington DC, USA.

Lankatilleke, L., 1986, 'Training and information for institutional development for the implementation of the Million Houses Programme of Sri Lanka', *Habitat International*, Vol. 10 No. 3, Pergamon Press, Oxford, UK.

Lee-Smith, D. & Memon, P., 1988, 'Institution development for delivery of low-income housing: An evaluation of Dandora Community Development Project in Nairobi', *Third World Planning Review*, Vol. 10 No. 3, Liverpool, UK.

Lewis, M. & P. Conaty, 2012, *The Resilience Imperative: Cooperative Transitions to a Steady State Economy*, New Society, Gabriola Island, BC, Canada.

Madden, D. & P. Marcuse, 2016, *In Defense of Housing: The Politics of Crisis*, Verso, London, UK and New York, USA.

Mason, P., 2016, *Postcapitalism: A Guide to Our Future*, Penguin, London, UK.

McCarney, P. (ed), 1996, *Cities and Governance: New Directions in Latin America, Asia and Africa*, Centre for Urban and Community Studies, University of Toronto, Toronto, Canada.

UN-Habitat, 2003, *The Challenge of Slums: Global Report on Human Settlements 2003*, (revised 2010), Earthscan, London, UK.

Index

Abdul-Wahab, R. 8, 110
Afghanistan, institutional development 147–8
Agenda 21 35, 97, 101n19
aguateros 138
Ahmedabad, India 7
aided self-help (ASH) 28–31, 32n7, 64
Aleppo, Syria 110, 131
Algeria, public housing 31n2
Allen, A. 98
Alwar, India, Shivaji Park S&S project 113, 122, 135, 140
Amman, Jordan, Urban Development Project 41
Andaraí favela, Rio de Janeiro 69
Angel, S. 125, 127
Antop Hill, Bombay (Mumbai), India 13
Archer, D. 96
Arnstein, Sherry 34, 60n3
Arumbakkam project, India 122–3
Ashaiman Women for Progressive Development (AWPD) 93
Asian Coalition for Housing Rights (ACHR) 112, 123, 150n1
Asian Development Bank (ADB) 89
asset management 136–7
Atkinson, A. 97, 98
Audefroy, J. F. 96

Baan Mankong Programme, Thailand 38
Baghdad, Iraq, Thawra City 136
Bairrinho and Grandes Favelas 70
Bakhtyar, B. 124
Banco Nacional da Habitação (BNH) 18
Bandra East, Bombay (Mumbai), India 22

Bangkok, Thailand, land-sharing 125
Bangladesh: Busti Baseer Odhikar Surakha Committee 111–12; incremental housing 125, 129
Banks, N. 112
barriadas 33, 117n5
barrios piratas 2
Beall, J. 91
Bebbington, A. 149
beneficiary selection 132–4
Bogotá, Colombia 2, 3–4, 12, 15, 15n2, 117n4; Ciudad Bachué 53–7, 135; Ciudad Kennedy 31; Las Colinas 49; Guacamayas 50–1; Plan Terrazas Programme 116; Policarpa 3–4, 12, 15, 15n2
Bolay, J. C. 114
Bombay (Mumbai), India: Bandra East 22; Buildings Repairs and Renewal Board 25, 44, 45; chawl buildings 26, 44–5, 60n10; City Development Strategy 89; incremental housing 109, 123, 125
Boonyabancha, S. 96
bottom-up schemes 93
Brandao, J. 74
Brazil: aided self-help 28; Banco Nacional da Habitação (BNH) 18; City Statut 148; Favela Bairro programme 63, 68–74, 79–80, 109, 110, 123, 132; land invasions 70; Minha Casa, Minha Vida (My House, My Life) programme 85; private sector 84–5; Rio Cidade 70; Santa Marta favela 73; solid waste and recycling 98

Brown Agenda 97–8
Bruntland Commission *see* World
  Commission on Environment and
  Development (WCED)
Buckley, R. M. 84, 90, 111
Build Together Programme, Namibia 75
Building Together project, Thailand 32n7
Burgess, R. 98, 110
Busti Baseer Odhikar Surakha
  Committee (BOSC) 11102

Caja de Vivienda Popular 50
Cali, Colombia, Plan Terrazas
  Programme 116
Cambodia: Phnom Penh 27, 123;
  savings schemes 113
Camplands S&S project, Jamaica 128
capacity building 145–6, 148
Caracas, Venezuela 5
Cemex 138–9
Centre for Research on the
  Epidemiology of Disasters (CRED)
  100n13, 101n15
Chana, T. 41
Chandigarh, India 116
Chant, S. 92
chawl buildings 26, 44–5, 60n10
Chennai, India, land-sharing 125
Chile, public sector intervention 18
Chirathamkijkul, T. 125, 127
Cities Alliance 89
citizen-building 113
citizen participation, ladder of 34, 60n3
City Development Strategies (CDSs)
  89–90, 110, 140–1
city forums 89
City Summit 35, 79
Ciudad Bachué, Bogotá, Colombia
  53–7, 135
Ciudad Kennedy, Bogotá, Colombia 31
climate change 93–7, 129
'co-production' of housing 9, 19, 35,
  60n5, 150
Coalition for the Urban Poor (CUP) 111
Cohen, M. 48, 58, 107, 108, 110, 121,
  132, 137, 140
Las Colinas, Bogotá, Colombia 49
Colombia 2, 3–4, 12, 15, 15n2, 117n4;
  aided self-help 28, 31; Ciudad
  Bachué 53–7, 135; Ciudad Kennedy

31; Las Colinas 49; Guacamayas
  50–1; Instituto de Crédito Territorial
  (ICT) 18; Plan Terrazas Programme
  116; Policarpa 3–4, 12, 15, 15n2
Colombian Communist Party (PCC) 3
Colombo Municipal Council (CMC)
  10, 11
Colombo, Sri Lanka 6, 9–10, 81n3,
  100; Gothamipura 99; Navagampura
  52–3; Wanatamulla (Seevalupura)
  46, *see also* Million Houses
  Programme (MHP), Sri Lanka
commodification 84
community action planning (CAP)
  68, 129
community contracting 131
Community Development Council
  (CDC) 11, 65, 67–8, 80, 81n5, 128
community land trusts (CLTs) 126, 127
community organisation 136–7
Community Organisation Development
  Institute (CODI) 38
community-based organisations
  (CBOs) 33–4, 67–8, 70, 72, 88,
  149; City Development Strategies
  89; community contracting 131;
  geophysical hazards 95; rented
  housing 115
compulsory purchase 124, 126
Conaty, P. 127, 150
conventional housing policies 18–25,
  30–1, 87–8, 99; rented housing
  114–15, *see also* public housing
Cooperative Housing Foundation
  International (CHF) 106, 132,
  135, 140
cosmopolitan development 91–2
cost cutting 28; sites and services
  (S&S) 48–9
costs of construction 32n8; aided
  self-help 28, 30–1
Côte d'Ivoire, rented accommodation 59
Cotton, A. 130, 131
cultural integration 91–2
Cyclone Nagris 96
Cyprus, energy policy 98

Dakar, Senegal 110, 140; Parcelles
  Assainies 47–8, 108, 132; sites and
  services 107

Dandora project, Nairobi, Kenya 40,
   41–2, 108, 112–14, 134, 135,
   137, 147
Danish International Development
   Agency (DANIDA) grant 63, 75, 77
D'Cruz, C. 112
decentralisation 34, 36–7, 38, 109
Delhi, India, city beautification 26
deregulation 37
'development promotion' 136
devolution 34, 37–40, 60n8-9, 88
Dhaka, Bangladesh, Busti Baseer
   Odhikar Surakha Committee
   (BOSC) 111–12
district managers (DMs) 65, 66
d'Monte, D. 125
drought 2, 94–5, 100n14

Earth Summit 35, 97
earthquakes 94–6, 101n15, 129,
   135, 136
economic development: incremental
   housing 112–14, *see also* finance
education 132
El Salvador: land cost and location
   121–2; La Presita in San Miguel
   29–30
empowerment 38–9, 145; bottom-up
   schemes 93
'enablement' paradigm 18
enabling policies xiv, 33–62, 87,
   145; case studies 63–82, *see also*
   participation
energy conservation 97–8
engagement, partnership paradigm 104
environmental sustainability 97–8
evaluation, sites and services (S&S)
   49–50

favelas 63, 81n11; Rio de Janeiro
   Favela Bairro programme 63, 68–74,
   79–80, 109, 110, 123, 132
Fernandes, E. 117n4, 148
finance: incremental housing 107–8,
   127–9; loans and mortgages 13; soft
   loans 116, *see also* savings
Fiori, J. 74, 85, 88, 111
flooding 94–5, 101n15, 129
food costs 121
Franceys, R. 130

Frediani, A. 47
freehold ownership 59
Freire, M. 89
'full cost recovery' 131
Fundación Salvadoreña de Desarollo y
   Vivienda Minima (FSDVM) 29
FUSAU-Integral 122

Gattoni, G. 110, 121, 140
gender needs and assets 92–3
geophysical hazards 93–7, 129, 133
George Town, Penang, Malaysia 23–4
Ghana: devolution 38; National Shelter
   Strategy 106; planning reform 135,
   140; women's rights 93
ghettoisation 91
Gilbert, Alan 59
Global Shelter Strategy to the Year
   2000 35
Goethert, R. 68, 129
Goetze, Rolf 33
Gothamipura, Colombo, Sri Lanka 99
governance: incremental housing
   111–12, 137; participation 36
Green Agenda 97–8
Guacamayas, Bogotá, Colombia 50–1
Gulshan-e-Shahbaz Scheme,
   Pakistan 43
Guyana, Low Income Settlements
   Programme (LISP) 121

Haiti earthquake 96
Hamdi, N. 68, 129
Haouch Mokhfi, Algeria 3
Hardoy, J. 5
Hasan, A. 131, 133, 137, 140, 141n10
homelessness xiv, 17; International
   Year of Shelter for the Homeless 35
housing authorities xiv, 17
'housing deficit' 21
Housing Development Department
   (HDD) 147
Housing Options and Loans Package
   (HOLP) 65
housing stress 132
Housing and Urban Development
   Corporation (HUDCO) 17, 28, 32n5
'housing as a verb' 58, 145
housing-need sub-groups 90–1
human resource development 146

Huruma, Nairobi, Kenya 6
Hyderabad Development Authority
(HDA) 42–4, 135–6
Hyderabad, Pakistan, Kuda-ki-Bustee
project 42–4, 130, 133, 135–6, 137

Ibis 75, 76, 81n14, 93
Imparato, I. 45, 59
incremental development 117n1,
145–50; components of support
120–44; informal Settlements 12–15;
strategies 104, 105–14
incremental improvement concept 130
India 17, 22, 109, 123, 125;
Ahmedabad 7; Antop Hill, Bombay
13; Arumbakkam project 122–3;
Chandigarh 116; chawl buildings
26, 44–5, 60n10; city beautification
26; City Development Strategy 89;
Kolkata 7; land-sharing 125; loan
eligibility 28; Maharashtra Slum
Rehabilitation Authority 124; rented
accommodation 59; savings schemes
113; Shivaji Park S&S project 113,
122, 135, 140; slum clearances 21,
25; Sustainable Chennai Project 98;
Tamil Nadu Slum Clearance Board
21, 25; targets 21; urban informal
landlords 117n8
individual property holdings 20
Indonesia: housing authorities 17;
Kampong Improvement Programme
113; Transmigration Programme 32n7
informal housing 149–50; costs and
benefits 15; geophysical hazards 94;
incremental development 12–15;
procurement processes 1–16; SWOT
analysis 14, 15, *see also* slums
infrastructure 88, 141n5; acceptable
levels 21; authorities engagement
9; energy conservation 98; Favela
Bairro programme 71–4; incremental
development 12–13, 109, 120, 122–3,
129–32; local participation 36; MHP
67; Oshakati 75, 77–8; private sector
137–8; sites and services (S&S)
48–9; slum upgrading 44–5
institutional development 147–8
Instituto de Crédito Territorial (ICT)
18, 53

Integrated Residential Development
Programme (IRDP) 83
integrated urban development 88
Inter–American Development Bank
(IDB) 71, 72, 89
internally displaced persons (IDPs) 92
International Year of Shelter for the
Homeless (IYSH) 35
Iran Urban Land Act 1979 126
Iraq, Thawra City 136
Istanbul City Summit 35, 79
Istanbul Declaration xiv

Jacob Lines Project 21
Jamaica, Camplands S&S project 128
Jenks, M. 98, 110
Jere, H. 113, 137
Jordan, Urban Development Project 41
Juba, South Sudan 41

Kampong Improvement Programme,
Indonesia 113
Karachi Development Authority 21
Karachi, Pakistan, Orangi Pilot Project
109, 131
Keivani, R. 126
Kenya: Dandora project 40, 41–2, 108,
112–14, 134, 135, 137, 147; Mathare
Valley 5, 6; Ministry of Lands and
Settlement 18
Khuda-ki-Basti, Pakistan 122
Kingston, Jamaica, Camplands S&S
project 128
Kolkata, India 7
Kuda-ki-Bustee, Hyderabad, Pakistan
42–4, 130, 133, 135–6, 137
Kumar, S. 59, 91, 115, 117n8

ladder of citizen participation 34, 60n3
Lagos Executive Development
Board 18
Lall, S. 113, 122, 135, 140
land 5; acquisition and law reform
123–6; banking 125–6; cost and
location 120, 121–3; incremental
development 120–1; subdivision
and sale 1–2; tenure and title 120,
126–7
land invasions 3–4, 7, 15n1; Brazil 70;
Sri Lanka 9

156   *Index*

Land for the Landless Programme,
  Philippines 32n7
land–sharing 124–5
land use zoning 19
landslides 95
Lankatilleke, L. 65, 146
law reform, land acquisition 123–6
Lee-Smith, D. 42, 108, 113, 134, 135,
  137, 147
Léna, E. 2
Lewis, M. 127, 150
Light (electricity company) 110
Lloyd-Jones, T. 96
Local Agenda 21 (LA21) 35, 101n19
Loradoni, F. 114
Low Income Settlements Programme
  (LISP), Guyana 121
Lusaka, Zambia 129–30, 134, 137

McAuslan, P. 124, 127
McCarney, P. 149
Madden, D. 84, 150
Madras, India, Arumbakkam project
  122–3
Magalhães, S. 71
Maharashtra Housing Board 22
Maharashtra Slum Rehabilitation
  Authority 124
Mahila Milan 93, 113, 123
maintenance: incremental improvement
  130; participation 33, 36, 40, 58–9;
  public housing 25
Malaysia: George Town 23–4; Public
  Low-Cost Housing Program 124
management: incremental housing
  108–10; participation 33, 34–45, 58–9
Manila, Philippines, slum clearances 25
Marcuse, P. 84, 87, 150
marketability 123
Marris, P. 18
Mason, P. 150
Mathare Valley, Kenya 5, 6
Max Locke Centre 137
Medellin, Colombia, Plan Terrazas
  Programme 116
Memon, P. 42, 108, 113, 134, 135,
  137, 147
Mexico: *Patrimonio Hoy* programme
  138–9; private sector 84–5; public
  sector intervention 18

Mexico City 121
Million Houses Programme (MHP),
  Sri Lanka 45, 52, 63–8, 79–80, 81n4,
  107–8, 114, 126–7, 128, 134, 146
Minha Casa, Minha Vida (My House,
  My Life) programme 85
ministries of public works xiv, 17
Ministry of Local Government and
  Housing (MLGH) 75, 79
Mitlin, D. 9, 35, 60n5, 93, 109, 113,
  123, 125
Moser, C. 60n6, 92, 93
motor vehicles 98
Mumbai *see* Bombay
Municipal Housing Department (SMH)
  70, 72
municipalisation 88
Myanmar, Cyclone Nagris 96

Nairobi City Council (NCC) 41–2, 147
Nairobi, Kenya, Dandora project 40,
  41–2, 108, 112–14, 134, 135,
  137, 147
Namibia, Oshakati Human Settlements
  Improvement Programme (OHSIP)
  45, 63, 74–9, 80
National Housing Development
  Authority (NHDA) 11, 52, 63, 64–5,
  67–8, 79–80, 81n5, 81n15, 99–100,
  114, 146
National Slum Dwellers Federation
  (NSDF) 93, 113, 123, 125
Navagampura, Colombo, Sri Lanka
  52–3
Nigeria: housing authority 18; Karu
  City Development Strategy 89;
  rented accommodation 59
non-conventional housing strategies
  33–62, 87–8, *see also* incremental
  development; participation
non-governmental development
  organisations (NGDOs) 34, 63;
  Ibis 75, 76, 81n14, 93; incremental
  housing strategies 105–6
non-governmental organisations
  (NGOs) 34, 88, 148–50; Brazil 72,
  74; City Development Strategies
  89; Coalition for the Urban Poor
  (CUP) 111; geophysical hazards
  95; incremental housing 108–10,

123, 125, 127, 128–9, 134; sites and services (S&S) 41, 44; Sri Lanka 65, 68; technical assistance 136; women's rights 93

Office d'Habitat de Loyers Moderes (OHLM) 47
One Lakh Houses Programme, Sri Lanka 32n7, 64
open access projects 133, 137
Orangi Pilot Project in Karachi, Pakistan 109, 131
organisational development 146–7
organised self-help *see* aided self-help (ASH)
Oshakati Human Settlements Improvement Programme (OHSIP) 45, 63, 74–9, 80
Oshakati Town Council (OTC) 75–6, 79, 81n14
Our Common Future 97
owner-occupiers 59
ownership 59, 136–7

Pakistan 140; Gulshan-e-Shahbaz Scheme 43; Jacob Lines Project 21; Khuda-ki-Basti 122; Kuda-ki-Bustee 42–4, 130, 133, 135–6, 137; Orangi Pilot Project in Karachi 109, 131
Paraguay, *aguateros* 138
Parcelles Assainies, Dakar, Senegal 47–8, 108, 132
Paris Agreement *see* United Nations Framework Convention on Climate Change
participation xiv; governance 111; non-conventional housing strategies 33–62, *see also* enabling policies
partnership approach 35, 104–19; incremental development 120–44
Patel, S. 93, 109, 123, 125
Patrimonio Hoy programme 138–9
Payne, G. K. 40, 126
Peake, L. 60n6
Peattie, L. 15
peri-urban land 121, 126, 138
Peru: *barriadas* 33, 117n5; Equal Opportunities Act 93; Villa El Salvador 15
Pervaiz, A. 109

Philippines: Land for the Landless Programme 32n7; slum clearances 25
Phnom Penh, Cambodia 27; incremental housing 123
Phonphakdee, S. 113
Plan Terrazas Programme in Colombia 116
planning: climate change 94; incremental housing 134–6; ownership 137; participation 34–7, 39; strategic 140–1; vacant land subdivision and sale 1–2
Platform for Action (PfA) 92–3
Plummer, J. 111
Policarpa, Bogotá, Colombia 3–4, 12, 15, 15n2
Praja Sahayaka Service 68
Premadasa, Ranasinghe 64
La Presita in San Miguel, El Salvador 29–30
private sector xiii, 149; incentives 83–6; landlords xiv, 117n8; rented housing 114, 115–16; S&S 137–40
privatisation 37
procurement processes, informal housing 1–16
profit-sharing partnerships 36
public consultation 34–5
public housing xiv, 87; conventional 83–6; reserves 125; subsidiarity 33, *see also* conventional housing strategies
Public Low-Cost Housing Program (PLHP) 124
public–private partnerships (PPPs) 35, 36
public sector: investment optimization 105; low-income group housing 17–32
Public Works Tradition 20–5

Rahman, M. 125, 129
Rakodi, C. 92
Ramirez, R. 47, 71, 88
ranchos 5
Rangoon (Yangon), Burma 22
refugees 92
renewable energy 98, 101n21
rent control legislation xiv, 20, 114; Sri Lanka 63–4

rented accommodation 24, 59, 91, 99, 114–16, 136; incremental housing strategies 105
returns on investment 132
'Rifle Range' housing project 23–4
Riley, E. 35, 67, 72, 79, 81n6, 105, 109, 110, 112
Rio Cidade (Rio City) 70
Rio de Janeiro, Brazil: Earth Summit 35, 97; Favela Bairro programme 63, 68–74, 79–80, 109, 110, 123, 132; Rio Cidade (Rio City) 70; Santa Marta favela 73
Rio Municipal Housing Department (SMH) 63
Rowbottom, S. 108
Ruster, J. 45, 59

Salavarrieta, Policarpa 3
Santa Marta favela, Rio de Janeiro, Brazil 73
Satterthwaite, D. 5, 112
savings: schemes 113; Sri Lanka 68
segregation 91
self-help 19, 28–31, 49, 58, 87, 110–11, *see also* aided self-help (ASH)
Senegal 110; Parcelles Assainies, Dakar 47–8, 108, 132; sites and services 106–7, 133, 140
Senghor, Leopold 48
services: administration 36; charges 36; provision 129–32, 141n5
Shack/Slum Dwellers International (SDI) 93, 112, 113, 150n1
Shivaji Park S&S project, India 113, 122, 135, 140
Shlyter, A. 130
Silas, J. 113
Simms, D. 8
Sirivardana, S. 68
sites and services (S&S) 19, 34, 40–4, 45, 47–58, 83, 99, 108; beneficiary selection 133–4; Brazil 70; incremental housing 106–7; infrastructure 129–32; location 122; planning 134–5; poor location 121; private sector 137–40; social solidarity 112; Sri Lanka 64, 65, 68
slums 17, 110, 149; clearances 25–8, 31n4; growth of xiv; of hope 33;

incremental development 13; Indian clearances 21, 25; Jacob Lines Project 21; Nigerian clearances 18; upgrading programmes 11, 19, 44–8, 83
social capital, incremental development 13–14
social development, incremental housing 112–14
social housing 87, 99
social mobility xiv
Society for the Promotion of Area Resource Centres (SPARC) 93, 123
soft loans 116
Sohail, M. 131
Solana Oses, O. 85, 111
solar energy 98, 101n21
South Africa 93; strategic development plans 38
South African Finance Linked Individual Subsidy Programme (FLISP) 83–4
South Sudan, Juba 41
squatting 3, 5–8, 110–11; authorities engagement 9; land-sharing 124–5; Phnom Penh 123; plot-by-plot 3, 5; Rio de Janeiro Favela Bairro programme 68–74
Sri Lanka 6, 9, 81n3, 100; 2004 tsunami 95; community action planning 129; Gothamipura 99; Million Houses Programme (MHP) 45, 52, 63–8, 79–80, 81n4, 107–8, 114, 126–7, 128, 134, 146; Navagampura 52–3; One Lakh Houses Programme 32n7, 64; Wanatamulla (Seevalupura) 46
Sri Lanka Women's Bank 68, 93, 113
standards of space and construction 21; cost cutting 28; sites and services (S&S) 48
Stein, A. 129
Stockholm, Sweden 126
strategic planning 140–1
Stren, R. 89
structural adjustment programmers (SAPs) 37
subletting, public housing 24–5
subsidiarity 33, 38, 40, 60n6, 60n 9, 87–8, 145; incremental housing 108, 129; partnership paradigm 104

subsidies 20–1; public housing 28
subsistence landlords 59, 91
sustainability: environmental 97–8;
incremental housing strategies 105;
urban development 88
Sustainable Chennai Project, India 98
Sustainable Development Goals
(SDGs) 88, 100n1
sweat equity 28, 131, *see also* aided
self-help
Swedish International Development
Cooperation Agency (SIDA)
128–9, 133
SWOT analysis 14, 15, 89
Syria: Aleppo informal settlements 110,
131; land banking 126

Tal al Zarazier, Aleppo, Syria 8
Tamil Nadu Slum Clearance Board
21, 25
taxation: incremental housing 131;
policies 19
Thailand: Baan Mankong Programme
38; Building Together project 32n7;
housing authority 17; land-sharing 125
Thawra City, Baghdad, Iraq 136
Tibaijuka, A. K. 85
Tipple, G. 135
traditional building methods 96
transferable development rights
(TDR) 124
tsunami 94–5, 101n15-6
Tunisia, Tunis City Development
Strategy 89
Turner, John F. C. 33, 58, 59n1, 117n5,
121, 145

United Nations: City Development
Strategies 89; Habitat 89; Habitat
2003 89, 106, 145, 149; Habitat
2005 116; Habitat 2007 131; Habitat
2011 94, 100n14, 129, 136; Habitat
2016 92, 99; The Habitat Agenda
xiv, 35; Habitat Global Land Tool
Network 125; New Urban Agenda
92, 99
United Nations Centre for Human
Settlements (UNCHS) 44, 81n15, 130
United Nations Children's Fund
(UNICEF) 65, 89

United Nations Conference on
Environment and Development
(UNCED) 35, 97
United Nations Conference on Housing
and Sustainable Urban Development
(Habitat III) xv, 88
United Nations Conference on Human
Settlements (Habitat I) 34
United Nations Conference on Human
Settlements (Habitat II) xiv, 35, 79
United Nations Development
Programme (UNDP) 75
United Nations Environment
Programme (UNEP) 89
United Nations Framework Convention
on Climate Change 88
United Nations High Commission for
Refugees (UNHCR) 100n5
United Nations Human Settlements
Programme (UNCHS) 75
United Nations International Year of
Shelter for the Homeless (IYSH) 35
United Nations Sustainable
Development Goals (SDGs) 88,
100n1
United Nations World Commission
on Environment and Development
(WCED) 97
United Nations World Women's
Conference on Action for Equality,
Development and Peace 92–3
United States Agency for International
Development (USAID) 28
United States Alliance for Progress 28
Urban Development Authority (UDA)
11, 65, 95
Urban Development Project, Amman,
Jordan 41
Urban Poor Development Fund 113
Urban Resource Centre (URC) 123

Valenzuela, J. 2
Van der Linden, J. 121, 122
Vance, I. 129
Vancouver, Habitat I 34
Vernez, G. 2
Villa El Salvador, Peru 15

Wakely, P. 8, 35, 67, 72, 79, 81n6, 105,
109, 110, 112, 127, 136

Wanatamulla (Seevalupura), Colombo,
  Sri Lanka 46
waste management 36
Weerapana, D. 64
Women's Bank 68, 93, 113
World Bank 49, 58, 135, 136; 1993
  Housing Policy 87; ASH projects
  29–30; City Development Strategies
  89; Dandora project 41; earthquake-
  proof construction 96; 'full cost
  recovery' 131; geophysical hazards

94; Jordan Urban Development
Project 41; Parcelles Assainies 47–8,
108; SAPs 37; Senegal S&S 107
World Commission on Environment
and Development (WCED -
Bruntland Commission) 97,
101n17-18

You, N. 98

Zambia, Lusaka 129–30, 134, 137

For Product Safety Concerns and Information please contact our EU
representative GPSR@taylorandfrancis.com
Taylor & Francis Verlag GmbH, Kaufingerstraße 24, 80331 München, Germany